LUMINOUS DEBRIS

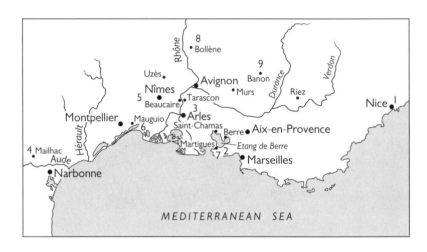

Archeological Sites Discussed in this Volume
Indicated by Both Place Names and Numbers

1. Terra Amata
2. L'Abri de la Font-des-Pigeons
   (Châteauneuf-les-Martigues)
3. Les Collines de Cordes (Fontvieille)
4. Le Cayla-de-Mailhac

5. *Oppidum* of Gailhan
6. Etang de l'Or (Etang de Mauguio)
7. La Pointe de l'Arquet (La Couronne)
8. *Oppidum* of Barri
9. Chastelard-Lardiers

Luminous Debris

REFLECTING ON

VESTIGE IN

PROVENCE AND

LANGUEDOC 🖎

Gustaf Sobin

UNIVERSITY OF CALIFORNIA PRESS

Berkeley   Los Angeles   London

University of California Press
Berkeley and Los Angeles, California

University of California Press, Ltd.
London, England

© 1999 by the Regents of the University of California

"Aquaeductus" and "West-Southwest" first appeared in *Heat*,
nos. 5 and 8; "Undulant-Oblique" and "On the Longevity of
Toponyms" in *Sulfur*, nos. 35 and 36; and "Terremare" in *Terra
Nova*, no. 4. The author wishes to express his thanks to the editors
of these reviews for their support and encouragement.

Library of Congress Cataloging-in-Publication Data

Sobin, Gustaf.
    Luminous debris : reflecting on vestige in Provence and
Languedoc / Gustaf Sobin.
        p.   cm.
    Includes bibliographical references and index.
    ISBN 0-520-21775-6 (alk. paper).—ISBN 0-520-22245-8 (alk.
paper)
    1. France, Southern—Antiquities.   2. Archaeology and
history—France, Southern.   I. Title.

DC607.4.S66   1999
936.4—dc21   99-20904
                                                        CIP

Manufactured in the United States of America

08   07   06   05   04   03   02   01   00   99
10   9   8   7   6   5   4   3   2   1

The paper used in this publication meets the minimum
requirements of ANSI/NISO Z39.48-1992 (R 1997)
(*Permanence of Paper*). ♾

For Esther & Gabriel,
With love

Contents 🖋

Acknowledgments 🖋

If any of the essays that follow help readers come to kindred realizations, then the limited ambitions of this book will have been fulfilled. I feel especially grateful to Eliot Weinberger, who first encouraged me to undertake such a project, and to the numerous archeologists and prehistorians of Provence who have been boundlessly kind, generous, and disinterested in helping me along my way. A number of the essays are specifically dedicated to those who made that "way" such an enlightening one.

Gustaf Sobin

Introduction ⚛

There's a breeze blowing through my work hut this morning. To keep my papers from flying about, I use, as a paperweight, a Neolithic stone axe head that I found years ago in a neighboring orchard. The axe head, slender as a trout and streamlined as a Brancusi sculpture, sits somewhat ponderously on top of a thick sheath of rattling white pages. The axe head is over four thousand years old. As for the rattling white pages, they're little more than so many day-by-day bits of scribble, fragment, outline: the disposable draft that authors inevitably accumulate. It's reassuring, of course, to see something as durable as a prehistoric artifact perched on top of one's own ephemera. Reassuring to see the past, in a sense, come to anchor all one's own, provisional, notation. Living as I do in a Provençal landscape rich with memento, with the materialized memory of so many past cultures, I've grown increasingly fascinated through the years with all the flint, ceramic, and serpentine that makes its way to the surface. Makes its way, fresh as dreams and remote as those founding societies, out of all that compounded subsoil.

The artifacts "speak" if we know how to "listen," if we learn how to interpret the operative details by which each might be identified. In this sense, the artifacts themselves are like words. They only await translation. In the essays that follow, I've attempted to translate a number of such words, phrases, relevant passages. I've drawn my materials from exactly those objects, those instances that I consider most meaningful in terms of our own particular existence today. In this respect, I am often reminded of a phrase of Roland Barthes. In it, Barthes describes his hesitation at the entrance to a Parisian cafe as he speculated whether the cafe contained anything "existential" at that given moment. I've chosen my materials herein exactly on that basis. What can a svelte, "willow-leaf" arrowhead tell us about ourselves? How do the ash grey potsherds of an Etruscan jug reflect—like opaque mirrors—some hidden aspect of our very existence? What exactly does the lunar crescent of a Bronze Age earring have to say?

I'd begun, years earlier, combing the surface of orchards, vineyards, wheat fields: whatever ground was subject to periodic plowings. The best season, of course, is winter. With the earth supple and the rainfalls abundant, the artifacts virtually ooze to the surface. I came to know whole patches of ground in which I could expect to find, say, traces of an outdoor Neolithic atelier (scrapers, blades, burins). Other spots secreted hunting tools (lance heads, javelin points), still others yielded a bounty of tiny, square-shaped, Gallo-Roman bath tiles—*tesserae*. Often these sites were no more than twenty or thirty meters in circumference, almost always within easy reach of still-available water sources and, invariably, sheltered from the all-dominant mistral. Flint, potsherd, the blue calcined bone of Neolithic game animals—all would abruptly disappear the very instant I stepped into the full force of that near-mythical air current. So many thousands of years after the fact, all vestige suddenly would vanish.

In only an instant, I would have stepped from the realm of "culture" to that of "nature": from artifact to scrub oak.

There's scarcely a moment of prehistory, protohistory, or early recorded history that hasn't left its trace in Provence's richly receptive earth. Often lying in as many as fifteen successive layers, these deposits range chronologically from the seasonal abodes of the earliest Paleolithic hunters to those of one's own vegetable garden, rife with the cracked faience and chipped marbles generated by one's own family. Between these two extremes, virtually every moment in human evolution has left its mark. From a bone bracelet of a Neolithic archer to a tiny bronze coin, the *viaticum*, once wedged between the teeth of a medieval ecclesiastic, history in these parts comes to illustrate itself.

If I myself have never dug—never participated, that is, in a proper, archeological expedition—I've spent a good deal of time practicing a parallel discipline, something I can only call "archival excavation." I've worked my way through the impacted tumuli of endless field reports, the theses (both published and unpublished) of doctoral candidates in archeology, the recorded addresses of prominent prehistorians at annual congresses. In every case, I've done nothing more than dig, scrape, sieve for the luminous detail. Indeed, I've had no further ambition as I rummaged through books, brochures, penned memoirs, and electronic printouts touching on everything from Mediterranean fossil pollens (palynology) to microtoponyms (paleo-linguistics) than the unearthing of those luminous details, those exemplary moments. In doing so, my research reading came to complement my field work: the *archiviste*, in a sense, elucidated the *flaneur*. Both, however, had been searching for exactly the same buried properties: the power—inherent in certain objects, certain instances— to generate reflection, reference, to serve as a kind of resuscitated mirror. Obscure, usually encrusted, more often than not illegible, these artifacts nonethe-less establish points from which we might situate our own existence today. Yes, across the millennia, the incised pictograph, say, of some protohistoric culture might serve potentially as a station, a vestigial marker for determining who, what, where we are, ultimately, at this very moment. "Existential," indeed. For the past, properly interpreted, clarifies the present: gives us—on occasion—startling glimpses of our own reality.

As we approach the end of yet another millennium, the insights that those glimpses provide grow all the more meaningful. Adrift in a world of semiotic vacuity, lost to ourselves in the midst of so much electronic overload, we've begun, as if intuitively, haunting museums, consulting archives, sifting through the apparent detritus of long-ignored vestige. Here in Provence, for instance, each village has generated its own historian; each dilapidated roadside shrine, its own restorer. In default of a viable present, we've come to valorize the past as never before. Propelled forward, we've turned, quite manifestly, backward, looking for the signs, signatures, and substantiating echoes of a world that un-derlies our own.

Each of the essays that follow enters, in varying degrees, a dialectic between those two orders of time. For myself, at least, the past per se holds little inter-est, and the present offers only the profound malaise of a culture increasingly devoid of the protocols of self-reflection. I've taken complete liberty in se-lecting, at will, specific objects, locations, and instances out of the past on the sole basis that they might serve, no matter how tenuously, that very dialectic. Nothing mattered in my choice of materials but the echoes, the mirroring im-ages they might provide, but the reverberations they might create.

The essays open with the study of a tiny Paleolithic windbreak, four hun-dred thousand years old, and they end with the examination of an aqueduct dating from the time of Claudius in the first century A.D. The essays are laid out in chronological order, although they make no attempt to "cover" that vast expanse of time. To the contrary, each represents nothing more than a brief *aperçu*—an exemplary moment—in that massive unraveling. The present volume spans a period from the outset of civilization to the Latinization of southern Gaul and covers an area approximately that of Roman Provincia, a vast administrative territory constituted by Augustus in 28 B.C. It includes a better part of what we've come to know today as southeastern France. Having lived in this area over the past thirty-five years, I've become, naturally enough, increasingly aware of its immense historical heritage, its vestigial wealth.

It is neither history nor vestige, however, that one first encounters upon arriving in Provence, but landscape, windscape. The wind is everywhere: in the twisted anatomy of the trees that one perceives in Van Gogh's paintings, in the architecture of its farmhouses that appear to crouch, even cower, against the long winter onslaughts of the mistral, in the delicately terraced olive orchards that face, resolutely, downwind. Downwind, too, lies the sun, that vast Mediterranean medallion. This very sun, I learned almost immediately, brings the almonds to flower in mid-February and the earth to crumble each August to a thin, insidious, funereal dust. It's the poignant world of Provence lying before one's eyes that one first encounters upon arriving. Faced with so much abundance, so much fruit and flower and golden, lichen-struck limestone, it's difficult to believe that this world conceals yet another beneath. That the lateral plane of our perceptions, in all its magnitude, keeps us from a deeper, more arcane set of cognitions below. That a *vertical* reading might indeed be possible.

There's a need today, perhaps as never before, to reestablish contact with that verticality: to feel ourselves rooted, not merely to the past in general but to our own specific moment within the past's tiered continuum. There is a need, in short, to situate ourselves in regard to our own evolving. Living as we do upon the uppermost layer of a profound compilation—one, that is, of wind, shadow, of voices buffeted by other voices—we need to feel that this residency has been "underwritten" by antecedents: that we, the living, are continuously accompanied by the presence, no matter how remote, of predecessors. That we're not, finally, alone.

PART I
Silex

Terra Amata 🪶

The beach cobbles lie there in little unruly heaps. Indeed, nothing seems to indicate any inherent arrangement in the way the stones lean one against another, as if toppled, at odd, apparently haphazard angles. There's nothing whatsoever to tell us that they'd been deliberately laid into place, over four hundred thousand years earlier, by Paleolithic hunters in a pathetic attempt to shield their pit fires against the high prevailing wind overhead. Nothing indicates their veritable nature but the fact that the cobbles themselves—loosely arranged in vague crescents, in curves no more than ten centimeters high and fifty centimeters wide—all face in a north-northwesterly direction. All happen to face, that is, the all-dominant, all-determinant air mass of the mistral.

We look on, amazed. Ours? we might ask ourselves. Really ours, these vestiges? The mark—no matter how makeshift—of some distant predecessor? Living as we do under one wind or another, but in the shelter of heated, heav-

*A four-hundred-thousand-year-old windbreak.
Photo courtesy Henry de Lumley, Musée de
Terra Amata, Nice.*

ily insulated houses, we look on, amazed by the fat pebbles in this archeological resuscitation, struck by the enormity of so much scant evidence.

Discovered quite by chance in excavating the foundations for a high-rise
apartment house in the suburbs of Nice, the site of Terra Amata has given us
a brief but luminous glimpse into a thoroughly obscure period of prehistory.[1]
The ancient site lies underneath ten meters of rubble, marine deposit, and ae-
olian sedimentation. Despite everything we've learned about Terra Amata
itself—it was occupied on a seasonal basis by itinerant bands of Acheulian
hunters (usually in late spring or early summer, according to pollen analyses

of the subsoil)—we're left with little material evidence regarding the hunters themselves. We have, of course, their artifacts. We even have an area that the archeologists have clearly identified as a worksite, within which the Acheulians would crack open the quartzite beach pebbles and create, with the constituent parts, their implements. But what of the hunters themselves? What of their size and physiognomy, not to mention their rites, their traditions, their *Weltanschauung?* Of these, nothing remains. Nothing but a small patch of barren earth at the very center of the worksite. There, surrounded by broken bits of beach pebble, in an area that the archeologists have described as "sterile," the tool makers must have squatted, chipping away at those round, ungainly volumes. Nowhere, in fact, is their presence at Terra Amata more apparent than in this manifest absence, this tight, earth-beaten patch of pure lacuna.

We're left, as ever, with residue, with the little that remains. In the Lower Paleolithic, this never constitutes more than a few scattered artifacts: traces of *Homo faber*'s attempt to survive an essentially hostile environment. So we return, over and over, to those piled cobbles, those pathetic little windbreaks, no wider than one's spread fingers and not much longer than a forearm. For these, unmistakably, were theirs. Cobble over cobble, these were what the hunters assembled for the sake of protecting the quick little scarves of their fires, the scavenged meats that they cooked, over four hundred thousand years ago, in the scooped hollow of the sand dunes. These were the tiny, fortuitous arrangements they made against the flat, lateral pour of that indomitable air current.

The mistral is still blowing. As we leave the museum in which the excavation has been meticulously preserved, we're struck by a blast of that blue air. Through the streets of Nice, the same wind blows unabated. We watch it catch, now, in the awnings of the outdoor cafes and billow through the taut canvas of the brightly striped beach cabanas. For us, of course, it's no longer an issue. We've long since learned how to shelter ourselves against every natural element; even more, we've learned how to harness those very elements to serve our own, ever-expanding needs. The wind—after how many hundreds of thousands of years?—rarely affects our lives. Like one of our own mass-produced appliances, we too have grown "windproof."

What, though, about those fires, we might ask? Those fires *within?* The subtle little flames each of us covets, not in the scooped hollows of a beach, but in the chambers of the brain or spirit or wherever we'd locate that tiny, flickering, unsubstantial glimmer that we've equated with life itself? The glow, say, of an early intuition? Or the sputtering embers of some still resilient memory? Are these fires any less exposed now than they were then? Any less vulnerable? And those cobbles, *our* cobbles, what we've laid into place along the rim of our consciousness in an unending effort to protect that fire, that glow, those embers: are they, in effect, any less provisional?

The wind today is still blowing, both inside and out. And if, at Terra Amata, we've lingered so long over such seemingly inconsequential artifacts, it's only because we have recognized—in cobble after teetering cobble—the extreme fragility of our own existence, displayed in paradigm. Found, among so much brute material, metaphor befitting our own human condition.

What characterizes humankind is our ability to evoke absent objects;
to *re-present* them mentally.

GEORGES SAUVET, "RHÉTORIQUE DE L'IMAGE PRÉHISTORIQUE,"
IN *PSYCHANALYSE ET PRÉHISTOIRE*

Reading Prehistory ❧

THE SEARCH FOR ANTECEDENTS

In the beginning was the eolith. So, at least, we're told upon opening a dense
introductory manual to prehistory. *Eo* for dawn, *lith* for stone: in the beginning, at the outset of humanity, came the eolith, the dawn stone, a heavy pebble
that's remarkable for nothing but the apparent absence of any distinguishing
characteristics whatsoever. Yet there it is, described, analyzed, even pampered—
for all its anonymity—as our very first artifact. Ours, we find ourselves asking once again? Living as we do at the far—the opposite—edge of civilization, we look back and wonder. Ours, those cobbles? Those round, nondescript
volumes, scarcely chipped about their contours and subject to endless doubt
and speculation by the paleontologists themselves? Yes, we wonder. For, at the
very start, nothing can differentiate a pebble naturally fractured by intense thermal change from one deliberately crafted. Yet it's exactly there, at that very
point, in that precise instant of deliberation, that that virtual figure, *Homo habilis*, evolves into *Homo faber*, the artisan. It's the inaugural gesture, the first
irrefutable mark.

We read on. We're anxious for signs, indications, for some founding echo to our all-too-precarious existence, our so-called being here. Aren't we always, indeed, on the lookout for some kind of substantiating proof? Searching for antecedents as we enter, deeper and deeper, into the obfuscations of our own present? Archeological typology, we quickly learn, allows us to associate an artifact with a particular level of human development: to correlate, say, a chipped pebble with the cubic dimensions of a human brainpan; to affirm that such-and-such had been fashioned by so-and-so. Us, though, we ask ourselves? Really ours, these ancestors? we go on asking, incredulous over so much dubious relic, so much scarcely articulated rock.

Come, now, the first unquestionable "pebble cultures." Comes that of the Oldowan, 1.75 million years ago, with their archaic handaxes chipped in *two* directions. Here, at last, we can begin to recognize a logical design, a pattern, repeating itself in the midst of the mineral: a frequency which constitutes a human signature. In the Quarternary (beginning as much as 2 million years ago, according to certain estimates), the ice cap has come to cover nearly the entire continent of Europe. Adapting to this cataclysm, a new creature evolves. In the celebrated formula coined by Linnaeus, this hominid, "*loquax, bimanum, erectum,*" never stops developing as a rational animal. Page after page, millennium after millennium, we follow this creature's catatonically slow evolution as it manifests itself in its lithic industry. A third chip here, a fourth chip there, and the Oldowan handaxe gradually turns into an oval- or pear-shaped tool, roughly worked on two surfaces. Now even an untrained eye can recognize the handicraft involved. One culture succeeds another: the Acheulian, we're told, follows upon the Abbevillian, 1.5 million years ago. And, as it does, the handaxe grows thinner, finer; its pressure-flaked edges become ever more masterful. Archeologists have come to nickname these implements *limandae* after their svelte, fishlike appearance. Tens of thousand years had to elapse, however, for this evolution to occur. We find ourselves, as ever, confronted with the incommensurable.

Concurrently, we're led through a succession of glacial expansions and interglacial contractions—all, of course, phases of that single, overriding epoch: the Quaternary. These phases have each been given the sharp, Teutonic place names of their alleged points of origin. Mindel, Riss, and Würm, for instance, are all affluents of the Danube. On the other hand, the cultures affected—determined—by these glacial fluctuations have each been named after the archeological sites far to the southwest with which—in terms of cultural evolution—they've been associated. Abbeville, Chelles, Saint Acheul, Le Moustier, La Madeleine are but a few such eponyms. Our familiarity with those places (all in France) or, simply, the lilt of their names brings us no closer, however, to those lost cultures. To the contrary, a kind of desolation increasingly sets in as we read on. A jaw bone, a few teeth, a crushed femur: are these really *our* vestiges? *Our* biological remains?

Here we're at the mercy of not only the archeologists, but a whole army of specialists, each qualified in some particular area of prehistoric research. The paleogeologists, readers of rock and rubble, can determine exactly how and when a particular cobble, for example, took on the shape that it did. By its striations alone, these specialists can tell us whether the cobble in question has been exposed to sea, wind, fire, glacial pressures, or solar heat. Equally as well, they can interpret river deposits, analyze loess—a volatile, wind-driven sediment—or the solifluction effect on any particular gravel bed. As we read on, though, we seem to be going further and further astray in our search for antecedents, for traces of some human determinant with which we might, even tenuously, identify. And although we've just been informed that a strict correlation exists between, say, sea levels, glacial relics, and human artifacts, we feel, if anything, more removed than ever from any brief, albeit ephemeral, instance of self-recognition.

The paleobotanists, curiously enough, lead us even further astray. Prying fossilized pollen loose from the same stratigraphic layers as those in which worked tools or human bones have been identified, they relate one form of extinct life to another. More desolate yet, we listen as they tell us, for example, how deposits of a certain microscopic marine creature—the radiolarian—accumulating at a rate of one centimeter per millennium, constitute a perfect means of determining a particular moment in human evolution. The moment can be "located," we're told, in relation to the level of alluvial accretion in which it occurs.

Where are we though, we're forced to ask ourselves? Reading as diligently as we can, chapter after chapter, glaciation after glaciation, don't we run the risk of falling half-consciously into the chasms of prehistory itself? Slipping between two pages into some dismal abyss? Finding ourselves smothered by so many concretized blankets of sediment, glacial debris, stalactitic drippings? There's little, indeed, to retain us. In default of that founding echo, there's little to reassure us that *here*, in fact, is still *here*. The discovery of a skull—irrefutable evidence, we're told, of a new level in evolutionary development—does little to allay our anxieties. No, we could go on falling, readily enough, through so many pages of so-called substantiating evidence, conclusive fact. Quite clearly, the arrival of *Homo neanderthalensis* does nothing to help. With their low foreheads, massive, overwhelming brow ridges, and stunted chins, they bear, indeed, scarcely any resemblance to us whatsoever. And even if the archeologists are quick to praise the considerable technological advances made by this predecessor, it's virtually impossible—in an age of genetic research and interplanetary exploration—to appreciate those advances to their fullest. These hominids—born, we're told, in the relatively temperate climate of the third interglacial period, rife with elephant, rhinoceros, and hyena—came to acclimate themselves to the gradual arrival of the last glaciation. Driven by severe cold into caverns, they adapted their lithic industry accordingly. If the aboriginal handaxe (beginning with the eolith and culminating in the elegance of the Acheulian *limanda*) had been perfectly suited for the nomadic life of small hordes in relatively warm open country, flake tools—flint knives with finely retouched edges—came into use now for skinning and preparing game in far colder climates. As ever, a fresh set of material circumstances elicited a fresh technology. Rather than working a rough block of flint into a corelike implement, the Neanderthal could turn the residual flake—the waste product itself—into a ready-made tool of its own. This discovery, we're told, was nothing short of revolutionary.

We read on. We go on looking, as we've always looked, not so much for them as for ourselves, our own, obscure traces. Reading books, visiting museums, or simply stopping short before the vast, gold umbrella of some chestnut tree in mid-autumn, aren't we always, in a sense, looking for ourselves? A lonely species by nature, made even more so today by the loss of any commonly shared vision—any collectively accepted referent—we wander through galleries, archival tumuli, and archeological vestige, hoping to discover, at any given instant, the key, the tiny, metallic glint in the midst of our own shadows. Call it, if you will, the breath at the very heart of our own empty mirror.

We turn backward because there's nowhere else, finally, to look. Nowhere else to search for our own specific, instigating moment but through the caverns and peat bogs of a prehistory that continually escapes us. We go on, wading through the millennia, inspecting the scant evidence, hoping that a collarbone here, a chipped flint there, might give us some small inkling. We've been forewarned, however, that human evolution is rarely explicit. If indeed we can trace the immeasurably slow technological progress that so many unearthed artifacts attest to, we're still left with little or no idea of our predecessors as living entities. Even their skeletal remains are few and fragmentary throughout the early Paleolithic and most of the middle Paleolithic: throughout, that is, ninety-nine percent of human evolution. We have to wait until the very end of this seemingly interminable period—until the closure, that is, of the Mousterian, in about 32,000 B.C.—before we encounter the first full, fossilized skeletons. Are we, we might ask ourselves, turning necroscopic in our search for antecedents? More drawn, say, to the tibiae than the possible reconstitution of gesture, movement, reflection? No, quite the contrary. For we can only begin to reconstitute the veritable life of these predecessors when we're allowed to examine not the bones alone, but the manner in which they'd been prepared for ritual inhumation. The skeleton of a man, for instance, buried in a small rock shelter at La Chapelle-aux-Saints, his head facing east in a half-circle of stones, a bison's hoof for *viaticum* lying alongside, tells us more about our own hidden identity than any number of axes, blades, or scrapers. For here, at long last, we can begin to enter prehistoric thought itself. The bones, ironically, bring us closer now to the animate, the cognitive. In a distinct acceleration of human development that has both puzzled and fascinated prehistorians, we're given, quite suddenly, a wealth of evidence. We have, for example, the Moustier skeleton buried in a fetal position, its head resting for the past thirty-four thousand years in the fold of its right arm. Or we'll read of another skeleton: that of a nine year old discovered in southern Uzbekistan, his grave encircled with the horns of Siberian mountain goats. The skull of this child, significantly, shows the first unmistakable traits of a new level in human evolution, of a new creature: *Homo sapiens sapiens*. We're at the dawn, now, of the late Paleolithic. More meaningfully, we're at the very point of encountering a hominid we can not only clearly identify but acknowledge. We're on the verge of self-recognition.

The late Paleolithic, we're told, began abruptly with extensive human migrations out of the Middle East (alleged birthplace of the *Homo sapiens sapiens* or Cro-Magnon), accompanied by critical advances in cultural development. Emerging as they did in the last pulsations of the final glaciation (about 36,000 years ago in France), these new, rapidly evolving societies carved the antlers of their favored game, the reindeer, into beautifully tooled pins, chisels, and hunting points with finely cleaved bases. Across the hard tundra, they hunted mammoth and the woolly rhinoceros, capturing their quarry in pitfalls or, where the ground was too frozen, erecting elaborate overhead fall traps to snare those ungainly mammals. But, far more than by any technological achievement, these Aurignacians—as they came to be called—distinguished themselves pictorially. For the first time societies began painting and carving, representing in images what had gone, until then, undepicted. The earliest cave paintings date from this period: their bold outlines—silhouettes, really—were executed by torch-light in red ochre and black oxide of manganese, or carved, scratched, incised into the rock partitions themselves. Portrayed in profile and in all their vernal innocence, horse and bison, ibex and antelope seem to gaze across thirty thousand years of elapsed time with a purity of line that astonishes us today.

Is it "art," then, in its very first manifestations, that we so readily associate with? Is it the power of representation that furnishes us—at long last—with that founding echo, that establishing fact? With the flush of self-recognition? Let's indeed look closer. What, exactly, has found expression in these earliest graphic gestures? Is it the huge underbelly of the bison itself? Its gait, its carriage, the way its head seems buried in the massive heft of its shoulders?

No, we might readily respond at this point, it's none of these. The mammal, despite its figuration, hasn't been portrayed or replicated as much as conjured—graphically summoned—as a metaphysical entity. It's not, indeed, a representation we're admiring here, but an invocation: not a beast that's been depicted, but a *wish*. We might well imagine that the artists themselves, confronting the immense emptiness of the tundra in relation to their own dire circumstances, didn't paint what they saw but what they needed: the inherent power they might magically appropriate from those migratory game species that, otherwise, lay well beyond their reach.

In short, we're in the presence of an articulated absence, or, more exactly, of an interval that seems to span the space between the manifest and the imagined, to oscillate between the *here* and the *there*, the *now* and the ever-imminent *then*. Between, that is, desire and gratification, supplication and response. Does anything more fully characterize our own true nature? Our spatial dimension? We are creatures, indeed, of interval, of innate longing. Locked into an ongoing instant of continuous projection, we, as *Homo projectivis* (if such a neologism can be permitted), finally come, now, to the point where we can claim ourselves. After so many pages of text, covering so many ill-defined millennia of human development, we begin, at long last, to recognize ourselves in these first invocations. Page after page, illustration after illustration, we become, ironically enough, visible to ourselves in the same instant that we acknowledge those who depicted—for the first time, in still-hesitant outlines—the invisible. As we do, our mirror, quite suddenly, comes to fill.

The First Hunters and the Last 🦅

It's where the fields began to narrow on either side of a tight, rock-bound canyon that I'd find them. Arrowheads, javelin points—they'd lie scattered over the otherwise empty ground (especially after the winter rains) in a perfectly random manner. They couldn't, therefore, be associated with some prehistoric site, couldn't be considered, say, the emanations of some clearly delineated Neolithic settlement. No, given the absence of any other form of artifact (particularly ceramic) and the variable distance between one hunting implement and another, their presence—archeologically speaking—could only be qualified as "eccentric." But was it, in actual fact? Couldn't some relationship be established between the implements themselves and the gully just beyond? Couldn't something be learned from the fact that the frequency of my "finds" would increase in a clear, if sporadic, manner as I approached the canyon itself?

Here, I'd learned to read landscape as never before. Learned to interpret, as a text of sorts, the muffled dialectic that exists, occasionally, between a specific place and its history: between a patch of earth, say, and whatever vestige it happens to exude of some past human culture. Here that vestige proved to be immensely eloquent. Judging by the artifacts themselves, I was dealing with a period of time that ran from the late Magdalenian, clear through the Neolithic to the very edge of the Bronze Age. In other words, I was dealing with the material evidence of hunting societies that spanned a period of no less than eight millennia, beginning with a moment twelve thousand years earlier.

Why here, though? I'd answer my question soon enough, for the response was all too evident. "Here," I came to realize, was a naturally endowed wedge for capturing game: a narrow, narrowing, funnel-shaped passage for running them down, cornering them within that tight limestone corridor. For a distance of at least a hundred meters it offered no shelter, no trees, no escape path whatsoever. Over the millennia, it had provided hunters, clearly enough, with an ideal ground for bringing their quarry to bay.

Twelve thousand years. The mind either balks at the immensity of such a figure or grows giddy contemplating the abstract expanse of so much elapsed time. There's nothing abstract, however, about the artifact itself: it might be a long, slender arrowhead in the form of a willow leaf lying in the palm of one's hand. Almost as long as the palm is wide, it's every bit as tactile, tangible as one's own pocket knife or fountain pen. Twelve thousand years suddenly seems to contract, to conflate into a single, glistening instrument. Like a lost word, a hieroglyph from some distant language, the artifact demands careful scrutiny, not just mere curiosity. It wants to be read.

Here, in brief, is a summary description of a few such artifacts from this location. I've chosen them for their value as specimens—as typological archetypes—and arranged them in chronological order. This order in no way reflects the material circumstances in which I found them, spread out over several hectares of ground and covering a period in my own life of over fifteen years. It simply represents a sampling of the times I'd go out "silexing"—as I came to call it—after a day's work as a writer, and find myself, once again, scanning the empty expanses before me, scouring the ground for a second set of stray vocables, lost nominals.

A SHOULDERED, LAUREL-LEAF POINT *(POINTE À CRAN)* PRESSURE-FLAKED OVER BOTH SURFACES.

The "shouldering"—the tapering of the flange for the sake of its hafting—almost invariably indicates the Magdalenian. Most likely, too, this particular piece had been mounted on the tip of some long, slender javelin or lance rather than on the shaft of an arrow, for bow and arrow appear at a somewhat later date. We're still in the late Paleolithic, in the twilight of the last glaciation. Itinerant hunters, traveling in small, compact groups, supplementing their game foods with roots, wild honey, acorns, and larvae, still employ propulsors for sending their harpoons and assagais—heavy implements—flying though air. They still employ javelin points such as this one as they move— as if in symbiosis—in the wet tracks of the very last retreating reindeer.

A TRANSVERSE, TRAPEZOIDAL ARROWHEAD OF TINY, MICROLITHIC DIMENSIONS.

I might have missed this artifact altogether (and how many others, quite similar) if I hadn't seen its likeness illustrated in archeological manuals or displayed behind dusty glass showcases in local museums. These first true arrowheads are, in fact, remarkably inconspicuous. Not only small and relatively asymmetrical, they were executed with a total disregard for appearance. In short, they don't "look like" arrowheads. Nonetheless, these tiny armatures (weighing two grams on the average), mounted on die-straight branches of hazelwood and shot from the earliest sprung bows, could slice air at the rate of thirty meters a second. They'd tear—rather than pierce—the flesh of their prey; as such, they've come to be classified as trenchant or sectional weapons. Who, in fact, crafted these curious, trapezoidal shapes? We learn that they belonged to a people—an entire civilization—caught in a slow but inexorable process of transformation. Moving from a nomadic existence to the first, archaic forms of a sedentary culture, these people, who emerged in the Mesolithic (9000–6000 B.C.), enjoyed the outset of a temperate climate not altogether different from today's. Simultaneously, they saw the arrival of a flora and fauna that would have remained to this day, had we not over the past thousand years disrupted our ecosystem to the extent that we have.

AN EXCEPTIONALLY LONG, ALMOND-SHAPED ARROWHEAD, PERFECTLY BISYMMETRICAL, SHOWING TRACES OF THE ORIGINAL RESIN WITH WHICH IT WAS LIGATED.

We've clearly entered, with this armature, the Neolithic, and so moved from the trenchant to the penetrant. As to the arrowhead's exceptional length, this can be related, readily enough, to the site itself. If, in the surrounding hills, I found arrowheads that never measured more than three or four centimeters, here I found points of the exact same facture that were nearly twice that length. The difference in dimension could only be attributed to their essential difference in function. If, in the hills, rabbit, hare, fox, and game birds were the traditional quarry, here in this natural limestone passage it was boar, wild oxen, and deer—driven down from the heights—that were tracked and cornered.

In both cases, the length of the point was perfectly commensurate with the weight—the bulk—of the game pursued.

Curiously enough, we've entered, with these beautiful armatures, a period in which the hunt no longer constituted a primary source of sustenance. Having come to settle in small agrarian communities, Neolithic people would depend increasingly on the harvest of their own crops and on domesticated cattle. According to osteological analyses, the bone remainders of wild animals would usually account, now, for less than ten percent of the total faunal deposits. One can only imagine, however, that game remained (as it does today), if not a necessity, a prized delicacy of the very first order.

AN ARROWHEAD IN RIPPLING, HONEY-BROWN, ZONED SILEX,
BARBED AND TANGED TO A PROFILE THAT'S OFTEN COMPARED
TO THAT OF A CHRISTMAS TREE.

With implements such as these, we've reached the apogee of flint making. At this level of technical proficiency, we know that "the end is near," as one archeologist has put it.[1] Perfection, after all, can only edge toward its own exhaustion. Soon, very soon, the last moments of the Neolithic (labeled, rather misleadingly, as the Chalcolithic: 2500–2300 B.C.) would produce the first trickle of a new, imported weaponry, pounded out of a hitherto unknown substance: bronze. Soon, the stone mallet and amorphous flint core would be supplanted by hammer and anvil; the open-air industry of knapping would give way to the smoke of so many blazing forges.

If I never found bronze arrowheads myself, it was due to both their extreme rarity and my own mischance. I'd simply never been lucky enough. On the other hand, I'd managed to collect a considerable amount of flaked prehistoric hunting tools within a clearly delineated area. That area, I should add, didn't include the limestone passageway where the arrowhead would have been re-cuperated from the viscera of the felled animal; they were found, rather, on either side of that deadly passage. There, on either side, the point might have easily gone astray or been dragged into the surrounding undergrowth by a wounded mammal seeking shelter.

Words, I called them. In my own need to read landscape—cultural land-scape—as text, I'd sought out whatever vocables, mute ideograms, I could find. But was my analogy justified? Wasn't an arrowhead, within that irreparably lost grammar, less like a word than an instance of punctuation, most particu-larly that of the hyphen? A hyphen that had miraculously survived each of the two terms it had once united: the hunter, that is, and the hunted? Wasn't I hold-ing, in the palm of my hand, a handsomely pressure-flaked connective between two dissolved signifiers? Two totally divorced entities?

I was dealing, after all, with a period of time in which game was plentiful and human population slight. It was, in Marshall Sahlins's words, an age of abundance, that of an "original affluent society."[2] Never again would nature be so bountiful; never again would earth supply humankind with such a seem-ingly inexhaustible storehouse of meat, fish, wild fruits. The image of Eden—ecologically speaking—was far more than allegorical. The woods abounded with rabbit, roe, red deer, and boar, and in the foliage overhead shuttled snipe, woodcock, partridge, and dove. Yes, an Eden of sorts that existed—as Edens always do—in an immensely delicate, infinitely precarious balance between giver and given, provider and provided.

Today, it's difficult to believe that such a balance ever existed. As I'd take the path down to that prehistoric hunting ground, especially in winter when the fields had just been plowed and were already sprouting with fresh artifacts,

I would hear hunters—the very last hunters—crying out to their dogs. And I'd hear the dogs, too, their goat bells tinkling down out of the hills as they sniffed the wet grasses before them.

"*Cerca, cerca,*" I'd hear. "Keep looking," the hunters would cry out in Provençal as, from time to time, they came into sight, empty leather pouches slapping flatly against their flanks. "*Cerca, chin,*" they'd cry out as they followed the edges, now, of those freshly plowed fields, the blue barrels of their shotguns glinting metallic over one shoulder or lying prone in the crook of their forearms. It was, of course, a vacuous enactment, an empty ritual. For there is nothing left now to hunt. On the hunters' part, it has become, each autumn, nothing more than a ceremony that each performs, driven, no doubt, by some deep, vestigial instinct. Call it, if you like, a genetic tick arising out of some immemorial codification. For not only has the country been hunted out, the massive—abusive—use of insecticides has so totally upset the ecological balance that the remaining fauna has either fled or perished. This particular Eden has turned into a gameless wasteland.

Occasionally, of course, one might still hear of some passing *gibier*. Last winter, for instance, a boar was downed in these very same fields. Its innards, apparently, still contained traces of the rice it had last fed on, escaping—far below—the flooded estuary of the Rhone. But even then, as one hunter remarked, its hide was a good deal "pinker than black." Like most game today, it had been domestically bred. One might make the same observation in regard to the rare partridge, pheasant, or hare. Freshly released from the wire-webbed cage of some breeder, it no longer possesses the natural instincts—or savor—of its species. It makes for easy prey and yields little more than its own somewhat tasteless flesh. As for the wild rabbits, they're afflicted, more often than not, with myxomatosis, and they die from something far worse than buckshot. The hunter today roams through woods and along the edge of fields that have long since relinquished all claim to natural habitat. Even the trees seem little more, now, than decorous props for an irrepressible, all-invasive technology.

I'm not suggesting that one need return to the Neolithic to rediscover some kind of natural equilibrium, for game in Provence remained relatively abundant until quite recently. I only wish to invoke a golden age in which wildlife was bountiful, and nature—a nature not only respected but venerated—provided for every basic human necessity. It was a time in which societies, living in relatively small numbers, enjoyed a perfect surfeit of sustenance; a time in which humankind—*unhampered by humankind*—knew plenitude.

"*Cerca, cerca.*" As I would scour the surface for artifacts, searching for traces of those first hunters, I would hear, in the distance, the petulant little cries of the very last. Hear the goat bells of their dogs as they rushed this way, then that, flaring out over the broken ground in search of some last surviving spoor. "Keep looking," the hunters would cry out. "*Cerca lou lapin,*" they'd call, entreating as they did, in that nearly extinct idiom of theirs, the very last escaping game. By eleven each morning, I knew, their hunting satchels would already be jammed with simples, wild chicory, *salades de champs*. And, at noon sharp, they would unload their shotguns—more out of outrage than cruelty—on anything that moved: crow, magpie, squirrel. Look—but for what? There was virtually nothing left, now, to look for.

If I'd come to read the aboriginal arrowhead not as a word but as a kind of hyphen drawn between two discrete quantities—between society and nature, the bestowed and the bestower—the connective itself implied agreement, reciprocity, trust. It implied a contract of sorts in which a lesser entity (ourselves) was granted permission to subsist upon the bounty of a greater entity (nature).

As a contract, alas, it has long since been broken. Subtle, immensely delicate, and perfectly determinant, it has left nothing today but scattered artifacts. Left nothing but those narrow, pressure-flaked flint weapons that once sliced air at thirty meters per second, conflating—as they did—the two indispensable terms of our very existence. Reciprocal signifiers—it's not altogether certain that we can survive without them.

Neolithicizing Provence 🦅

CARDIAL, A CULTURE THAT CAME FROM THE SEA

It came in a wave, in a steady, immensely slow, earth-lapping undulation. There was nothing to stop it. In what has often been called the single most significant moment in human evolution, the arrival of the Neolithic (in Provence as a bit everywhere) would mark the end of one level of development, based essentially on hunting in small, nomadic groups, and the outset of another, devoted to farming and stock breeding. In increasing numbers, societies would establish themselves in their first fixed communities. This immense evolutionary step was due, in part, to ceramics: to the invention of the earthenware container. In allowing populations to store, it allowed them to settle. In Provence, they would settle first in grottoes close to the sea. The earliest of these, L'Abri de la Font-des-Pigeons at Châteauneuf-les-Martigues, has offered archeologists a wealth of information.[1] From its lowest stratigraphic layer, it has yielded— along with the oldest documentary evidence of ceramics in territorial France— the eponymic decor by which these ceramics might be identified.

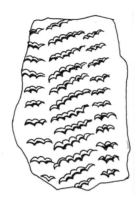

A fragment of cardial ceramic ware.
Drawing by Gabriel Sobin.

Named Cardial ware after the seashell—the common, heart-shaped cockle (the Latin word is *cardium*)—with which it was imprinted, this earliest pottery celebrates its own origins. It came in a wave, as if emerged from the sea, from a sea already rife with oars, with sails, with the produce of emergent cultures bearing the first unmistakable marks of a Mediterranean homogeneity. Similar "impressed ware," dating from the same period, has been discovered in sites as apparently disparate as Corsica, Liguria, and Spain. In each case, the ceramics bear the characteristic signature of those initiating cultures. The imprint itself was obtained by pressing the serrated edge—the teeth—of the cockleshell against the yet unfired contours of the ceramic vessel. It left, as impression, a brief, vibratory squiggle suggesting liquid, liquidity, the shimmering of fluid, say, over the flanks of some stout, round-bottomed storage jar.

Curiously enough, this first manifestation of the Neolithic in Provence would remain water oriented throughout its two-thousand-year duration. In permeating the interior, it would follow the course of rivers, establishing itself in small communities on either bank. Not once would it settle in the hinter-lands, beyond. Reflexive by nature, the Cardial culture seemingly advanced with its face facing backward, never, at any point, renouncing its eminently marine—eminently Mediterranean—origin. Was this due to some basic, metabolic need on the part of those initiating societies? To a diet that required, say, a certain salt- or freshwater nutrient? This is altogether possible. In any case, these first Neolithic populations would continue to practice, along with agriculture and stock breeding, the essentially atavistic activities of fishing, trapping crustacea, gathering gastropods. Indeed, as they moved inland in that slow, wavelike mi-gration of theirs, they'd leave—as vestige—not only their shell-impressed pot-tery, but so much scattered sea token, marine memento. In Avignon, for in-stance, along the banks of the Rhone, a worker operating a steam shovel in the 1960s discovered, quite by chance, an early Neolithic skeleton: an inhumed corpse in partial anatomical connection. Identified as that of a male in his mid-thirties, its skull was coiffed in a delicate hair net of perforated seashells. This net, a mesh really, beaded with Dentalia and Columbella, constituted an es-sential part of the defunct's funerary wardrobe, along with its seashell belt. Un-mistakably Cardial, it offers eloquent testimony to a culture that—for all its revolutionary achievements in the fields of agriculture, animal husbandry, and ceramics—remained, nonetheless, profoundly *reminiscent*.

Even more remarkable, however, was the rate at which that wave—that slow undulation—would unfurl. For we have archeological evidence that the Cardial, in its infiltration of riparian Provence, took nearly a thousand years to travel from its initial site within close reach of the coastline, Châteauneuf-les-Martigues, to that of its ultimate station northward, Courthezon, in the Vau-cluse.[2] The distance between these two points amounts to no more than eighty-five kilometers along a straight line. Even if we double that figure, however,

Cardial inhumation: note the traces of a funerary
belt made of seashells about the subject's waist.
Photo courtesy Gérard Sauzade.

to allow for the fact that this culture would have followed the sinuous contours of both the Rhone and its confluent, the Ouvèze, we're still brought to a startling observation. It took nearly a millennium for the Cardial to travel a distance that now can be driven in a bit more than an hour, and dialed—like anywhere else in the world—in a matter of seconds. We have grown so used to living in a violent contraction of space and time that, in comparing these two diametrically opposite cultures—ours and theirs—it's not the speed at which we're presently traveling that so astonishes us, but the apparent languor—immobility—in which they, the first Neolithics, seemed to indulge.

Two suppositions come immediately to mind. Whoever they were (and we know, in fact, painfully little), we may safely assume that they weren't motivated by gain, acquisition, conquest. They may, indeed, have lived very much like certain Californian tribes before the Spanish conquest: in relative autonomy, with mutually respected boundaries that kept each tribe, as if circumscribed, inside some naturally defined perimeter. Within that perimeter, however, lay an abundance of cultivatable soil and a seemingly inexhaustible store of natural resources. Living in relatively small numbers in the midst of so much bounty, these societies had no real need to expand. They self-sufficed. Their culture, consequently, didn't penetrate the interior as much as seep, trickle—traveling at exactly the speed at which recipient populations chose to absorb, to assimilate, their innovating techniques. Our first supposition, we discover, has led ineluctably to our next. Not only was Provence "neolithicized" without the least trace of conquest, cultural imposition, *mainmise*, but the whole process occurred—over that very period of one thousand years and within an area not exceeding a thousand square kilometers—at a cadence of assimilation entirely determined from within: by, that is, each of the collectivities involved. It should be noted that these recipient peoples were still living, for the most part, in the late Mesolithic: hunters and gatherers, they had continued to survive, at a subsistence level, in small, semi-nomadic communities. Almost entirely autarkic, they would undergo acculturation at a rate that varied according to the volition of each particular society. One after another, however, they came to cultivate their own fields, breed their own cattle, settling—for the first time—into fixed, agropastoral communities.

What happened, we might ask, to the Cardial culture, to those earliest Neolithic societies in Provence? They had marked the first—albeit hesitant—steps in what V. Gorden Childe called the Neolithic Revolution.[3] That revolution would gradually absorb the Cardial in its three-thousand-year peregrination, totally transfiguring society at every conceivable level. Caught in its acceleration, the Cardial would fade, give way—inevitably—to far more aggressive forms of acculturation, yield to forces far less circumspect. The mid- and late Neolithic in Provence would create the material conditions for an immense increase in food production. This increase would lead the way, ineluctably, to a proportionate rise in human population. One would be the *sine qua non* for the other. In turn, this sudden demographic expansion would generate in a relatively short period of time a whole set of fresh conditions of its own. Most especially, it would spell an end to those unquestioned boundaries. Under the pressure of that spreading population came—naturally enough—incursion, encroachment. Came, by the end of the Neolithic, border disputes, property squabbles, intertribal conflicts. Came, for the first time (at least to our knowledge), the manufacture of flint weaponry for the express purpose of warfare. How, we might ask, can archeologists make this distinction, given that the arrowheads used in these intertribal conflicts in no way differ from those employed in hunting? The material evidence speaks for itself.[4] At Roaix in the Vaucluse, for example, the production of flint armature continued to rise at the same moment that the hunt (according to modern analyses of the faunal deposits) fell to an all-time low. There remained for most of those svelte, symmetrical projectiles but one possible quarry.

We might infer from the given evidence that these first verifiable instances of human conflict created in the consciousness of these tribespeople a heightened sense of the imminent, the impending, of the dangers that lay—permanently now—at the very heart of the temporal. That bit by bit societies had begun living *against* rather than *within*: living at the risk and peril of their own fellow creatures, as opposed to the inscrutable mercy of natural—call them supernatural—forces. That bit by bit the temporal had begun substituting itself for the spatial: the perception of the immediate for that of the boundless. The rustling undergrowth for the radiant cloud.

None of these profound transformations in human consciousness would have been possible, however, without the technological achievements that immediately preceded them. Of all those achievements, the invention of ceramic ware would determine those transformations more, perhaps, than any other. Indeed, it would come to alter humanity's vision of the world altogether. Quite aside from the obvious advantages that ceramics afforded—to store food supplies against their very source, a capricious nature, that is—they gave societies the means to quantify what they'd always considered, until then, unquantifiable. They could count what they'd always considered, until then, uncountable. Humanity would begin laying down a reign of numbers over the fields of the given, the naturally bestowed. With so much well-stocked inventory, it could begin taking its distance from the unpredictable workings of invisible agencies. Bit by bit, it would come to separate itself from the inseparable, from that level of consciousness that admits to no severance between the animate and the inanimate, between the self and the inextricable fabric of so much surrounding phenomena. Increasingly, Neolithic societies would come to live under the privileged sign of number: a number by which they might not only measure but temporize, creating—quite unwittingly—the very conditions for their own ineluctable alienation. Bit by bit, they would come to take their distance from those earliest rocks, winds, stars, those immeasurable expanses of which they once felt themselves an integral part. Humankind would enter, now, a vision of existence based more and more on quantification and its immediate corollary: the temporal. At the far end of that vision—at the very extremity of its long corridor—the mirror of death would await those evolving populations.

It came in a wave: in a steady, immensely slow, earth-lapping undulation. It came as if despite itself, prescient—already—of the overwhelming effect it would have upon everything it touched. Wrapped against its own momentum, as if coiled in a futile attempt to check or—at least—minimize the extent of its own influence, it would carry, in its invisible chambers, the very memory of its lost origins. In the thousand years it would take to travel no more than a hundred and seventy sinuous kilometers, it would carry—imprinted on its ceramic vessels or perforated to adorn the bodies of both its living and its dead—the ubiquitous signature of the seashell. Mementos, indeed. Against the unraveling of what we'd come to call an irreversible evolutionary process, the *cardium*—the simple, pink-hearted cockle—would bear singular witness.

for Jim Clifford

Archeological Rhetoric 🖋

No more than a century ago, Provençal archeologists would go out on Sunday excursions, as they'd call them. Entering into "delectable valleys" (*vallées délicieuses*), they'd follow the "fanciful curves" (*sinuosités capricieuses*) of river beds in search of prehistoric artifacts: whatever those "archaic societies" (*antiques populations*) might have left in way of vestige. If the language of those nineteenth-century erudites remained unfailingly lyrical, their vision, nonetheless, expressed a remarkable sensitivity to environment, to the specific qualities of place itself. Invariably, they'd associate their discoveries with the natural milieu in which they'd been found. Wind, shadow, the orientation of certain rock faces in regard to some specific stellar configuration would enter their reports. Nothing remained disrelated. Upon discovery, each artifact would immediately be assigned its place—rhetorically speaking—within the resonant fields of the associative.

As might be expected, however, that rhetoric was never more than ap-

Une excursion à Bonnieux et à Buoux

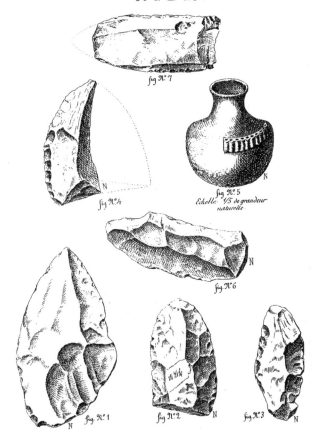

*An excursion to Bonnieux and Buoux: a
nineteeth-century rendering of artifacts. From*
Une excursion à Bonnieux et à Buoux:
Mémoires de l'Académie de Vaucluse, *1886.*

proximative. Read today in light of modern archeological terminology, it strikes one as vague, impressionistic, even—in terms of documentation— downright irresponsible. We're still at the outset, we should remind ourselves, of a recently discovered "humanism," as opposed to the ever more specialized, ever more applied "science" archeology would soon become. In moving from one to the other, archeology would coin a terminology of its own. Indeed, in the intervening century, one may not only follow the development of archeology as discipline, but—simultaneously—as rhetoric. One, ineluctably, would reflect the other. In reading a set of field reports in any form of chronological order, for instance, one has the impression of gradually abandoning an entire environment for the sake of an ever narrower, ever more explicative field of inquiry. Of going, within a relatively brief span of time, from watercolor to x-ray.

Hector Nicolas—to take an example—in filing his report from Avignon on 8 November 1884, would describe the flint tools he'd found in those delectable valleys: there, where so many "clear ripples" (*ondes limpides*) came to "ravish" (*ravir*) the banks in the continuous "throe" (*tressaillement*) of their passage. The tools themselves, alas, received far less evocative treatment. Some are described as having "no appreciable form" (*sans formes définies*) whatsoever; a flint armature—an arrowhead? a javelin point?—is rapidly dismissed as some "roughly executed" (*à peine ébauchée*) weapon of no discernible period.[1] We only need compare this passage with another, taken at random, from some present-day archeological study touching upon the same topological area. There, a particular artifact will be inventoried, for example, as follows: such and such a "mesial fragment of a blade(let) with proximal fracture due unquestionably to thermal action" will exhibit traces of "silica gloss on its scalariform edge-dressing interrupted, occasionally, by irregular flaking . . . ," etc.,

etc. The instrument itself, we learn, was fashioned out of a "quasi-translucent blonde silex" and discovered at such-and-such a square centimeter on "stratigraphic level 38" of such-and-such a site.[2] In comparing these two documents, one is struck, of course, by the qualitative difference in their descriptions. One soon comes to realize that this young discipline, in growing ever more precise, would create for itself an ever expanding taxonomy. As its field of inquiry narrowed, its terminology could do nothing but proliferate.

The focus of attention would come to fix itself almost exclusively on the artifact itself. Today, a particular flint tool, for instance, is first examined in relation to its raw material: the flint nodule or the matrix that once encased it. After preliminary study to determine the morphology of a "reconstituted lithic assemblage," an unworked nodule of local extraction will undergo "granulometric analyses" to gauge the frequency of "fracture propagation" under assumed working conditions. These analyses will be followed by others to measure the "elastic and isotropic qualities" of the mineral involved and its aptitude, finally, for knapping. We've come a long way from those Sunday excursions and the poetic résumés of that early Provençal archeologist, plucking artifacts like pastries from the entry of some "monstrous cave" (*caverne monstrueuse*). In no time whatsoever, we have gone from a single individual's immediate impressions to the thoroughly anonymous data of irrefutable, material fact.

After all those intense, preliminary analyses, touching on the inherent qualities and susceptibilities of its mineral composition, the artifact will then undergo a series of examinations to determine the technical aspects of its fabrication. Typometric, typological, and functional, the criteria for these examinations have grown increasingly exacting. For its edge-dressing alone, a given blade will be scrutinized to determine the precise angle at which its pressure-flaked dressing was executed. Even the scale of the flakes themselves ("long," "short," "invasive," "self-inclusive"), their morphological characteristics ("scutate," "scalariform"), the very cadence—rhythm—of their distribution, will enter an ever-expanding field of determinants. With each new determinant, we'll have—of course—a fresh description. The terminology only goes on growing.

Laboratory examination with the naked eye isn't enough, though; the artifact will inevitably fall subject to intense microscopic readings as well. At a low level of magnification, it will undergo "edge-damage analysis" to determine by scratch marks alone (its "stigmata") the *direction* in which it was originally employed, the *extent of wear* that it underwent, and, of course, the exact *function* it once fulfilled. These tests will invariably be followed by others under increasingly high levels of magnification. In "microwear analyses," for instance, through the use of scanning electron microscopes, bits of residue— vegetal fiber, phytoliths—will occasionally be detected along the edge, say, of some particular instrument. This detrital deposit gives research archeologists invaluable information in regard to the *materials* that this instrument once serviced.

Have we grown any closer, though, to those scant deposits? To so much scarcely perceptible matter? Indeed, in reading archeological studies, one has the distinct impression today that our means of detection overwhelm the vestigial materials that they've come to detect. We know more and more, it seems, about less and less. Victims, perhaps, of our very methodology, we've zeroed in on an ever narrowing field of inquiry. We've come to question, in ever more incisive terms, a body of material increasingly devoid of context.

Concurrent, now, with all the laboratory analyses come graphs, charts, "typometric diagrams" that trace—in sprays of minuscule dots—the displacements of a particular lithic manifestation. Called clouds, these sprays carry in their amorphous drift a whole microcosm of prehistoric data. Where, though, in all this processed information, are those lost societies? Where are those vanished cultures in the minutia of so many hyper-refined pictographs? Granted, archeology as "the study of human history and prehistory through the excavation of sites and the analysis of physical remains" (as defined by the *Oxford English Dictionary*) shouldn't be confused with metaphysics, with our own private need to affix an existential value onto each material insight. And yet, here we are, shuffling through the pages of that human history and prehistory, wondering, indeed, who those forgotten people really were. Well beyond the internal wars that archeologists wage over the increasingly finite questions of chronology and classification, we go on asking, too. As our own most distant reflections, we're curious to "unearth" the air that they breathed, the very sounds with which their rock shelters resounded, the lightning bolts in which they might have recognized the jagged signatures of an otherwise invisible spirit world. They escape us, of course. Escape us entirely. Our speculations, finally, are nothing more than the by-products of flair, instinct, intuition: our own, sensorial "reading" of so much extinct human landscape.

Has modern archeology, though, in its microsurgical approach to prehistory, come any closer, we might ask? As a science devoted to the study of human culture, has it taught us any more, in fact, than did those first, leisurely scholars who would amble out on Sundays in search of artifacts while remaining, all the while, unfailingly attentive to the contextual elements of place itself: the attributes—both palpable and impalpable—of a given historic environment? Nature, as Heraclitus wrote, loves to hide. So, too, does the veritable sense of so much apparently interpreted matter. Indeed, it might even be said that every fresh concentration of knowledge generates, ipso facto, a fresh dispersion. Nature—one might extrapolate—loves to flee.

Nicolas put it another way. In the opulent rhetoric of his time, he reported: "There where the mountain thrusts itself forward in immense, overhanging ledges, the shelters beneath defy all description. For it is there," he went on, "that the projecting, geological strata, hovering over their prodigious volumes would seem to protect those archaic societies from our very investigations."

"To protect those archaic societies from our very investigations." We go on investigating, though, don't we? Go on examining so much scant evidence for its least, elusive trace. Go on entering, in the ever narrowing field of a continuously expanding terminology, our own impacted data. The data, however, do not seem to bring us any closer.

Moon Goddess 🖎

SPECULATIONS ON A PICTOGRAPH

In every archaic culture, a grammar of images, of pictographs, precedes that of letters: the sign, or *sema*, is first of all pictorial. Even if these pictographs evolve with time into phonetic units—find themselves transformed, that is, into so many verbal signifiers—at first it is the pictures themselves that *speak*. Carved into wood, rock, deer's antler, it's the sign, the linguistic antecedent, that *signifies*. Having neither the aesthetic pretension of sculpture nor, as yet, the verbal attributes of the written character, it belongs to an intermediate idiom of its own.

Five kilometers northeast of Arles and only several hundred meters beyond the Abbaye de Montmajour, a series of such pictographs can be found scattered over open ground. Carved in limestone on flat, recumbent slabs or, in one case, upon the flank of a menhir, they each describe an inverted *U*. Down the center of that inverted *U* runs a prolonged dash. Taken together, the vaulted *U* and the vertical dash it encloses form the two movements—reciprocal

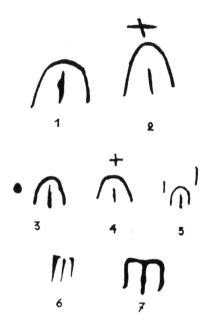

Carved pictographs from Les Collines de Cordes.
Drawing by J. Granier; courtesy Palais de
Roure, Avignon.

gestures—of a single, singular pictograph. This pictograph may or may not be accompanied by outlying dashes, crosses, cupules: signs that have traditionally been interpreted as stellar. As to the meaning of the pictograph itself, we have only what the archeologists would call working hypotheses. We may safely assume, however, that the sign, unmistakably female, represents the vulva and, as such, signifies birth, fecundity, perpetuation. It's not by chance that this immediate area, Les Collines de Cordes, is rich in hypogea: underground burial chambers carved in long corridors out of the surrounding rock.

Clearly the pictographs relate directly to the burial chambers themselves. For everywhere throughout the megalithic culture of this period, symbols of rebirth and regeneration accompanied the dead. Nowhere, we may safely say, was life represented in all its procreant magnitude more fully than in these late Neolithic burial sites.

Far earlier, though, in the midst of the Aurignacian (in about 30,000 B.C.), the inverted *U*-shaped pictograph had already made its appearance. Labeled "vulvaform" by André Leroi-Gourhan, it was often represented, painted or engraved, deep within the recesses of any number of late Paleolithic underground sanctuaries such as those at Abri Cellier and Abri Castanet. In the Cabinet des Félins at Lascaux, the inverted *U* of the vulva is repeated three times in a concentric, vibratory pattern, thus bracketing the vertical stroke mark of the vagina within. The form, of course, is ineluctable. In an iconographic rendering of the female anatomy, the pubic section—be it oval, triangular, quadrilateral, or claviform—could hardly be treated otherwise. Evidence indicates that Magdalenians would travel great distances to collect this very sign in the form of a seashell, a delicate bivalve known, appropriately enough, as a *cypris*. Named after Aphrodite, the Cyprian, its form bears a striking resemblance to that of a vulva. The sign itself must have constituted a privileged element in an alphabet of signs, be it carved upon the face of a wall or simply collected as a naturally endowed ideogram.

Here, though, in Les Collines de Cordes, we're no longer in the Paleolithic, but in the late Neolithic (about 3000 B.C.). Although graphically identical, the sign itself has undergone a fundamental symbolic change. Throughout both the Paleolithic and Neolithic, it signified, of course, fecundity. If, however, in the former period that fecundity was exclusively perceived in terms of the living (and most especially in regard to the propagation of the species), in the latter period it came to be associated with the regeneration of the dead. In the afterlife of the corpse, laid in fetal contraction within the *cella* of some chamber tomb, it suggested—we may safely speculate—rebirth and resuscitation, but in a world apart. Symbolically charged, the pictograph not only invoked that second world but indicated the way—the very passage—by which the dead might accede. Manifestly enough, the way was matricular.

It would be tempting to compare this relatively discreet sign with that, far more explicit, of the famous "Cuttlefish of Lufang" pictograph, carved upon the wall of a chamber tomb at Crach in the Morbihan, or the painted frescoes of that same sea creature as they appear at the palace of Knossos in Crete. The similarities are remarkable. Scarcely disguised by so many surrounding appendages, couldn't this cephalopod be the very signature of the vulva itself? What's more, can't we speculate that we're dealing, in each instance, with a moment in the late Neolithic in which lunar (and thus aquatic) divinities reigned over the consciousness of humankind? In which the diaphanous figure of the moon goddess herself still flooded the fields of the human psyche? Indeed, with these scattered pictographs in Les Collines de Cordes, we might well be witnesses to the very last moments of those "lunar-telluric-agrarian hierophanies," as Mircea Eliade describes them.[1] Soon, we know, these somewhat subliminal, if all-determinate, divinities will be replaced everywhere by male counterparts. Undergoing a steady process of "virilization," the mythologies of late Neolithic and Chalcolithic societies will gradually *solarize*: gradually abandon the discreet, somewhat esoteric signatures of the lunar divinities in favor of the ever more figurative, "activated" representations of the nascent sun gods. We're on the verge, now, of history. It's a time in which humankind would come to take increasing technological control over its natural environment. Along with farming and stock breeding, the advent of metallurgy (bronze and, soon after, iron) would permit societies to live with a growing sense of independence in regard to their immediate environment. In greater and greater numbers, agropastoral communities would spring up, developing, as they did, an increasingly hierarchical, increasingly male-dominated socio-religious mentality. Chieftains, now, would be consecrated upon death and treated as divinities, gods invested with the fecundating powers of the sun, as opposed to the germinal effusion of those far earlier "lunar-telluric-agrarian" goddesses whom they'd come to replace.

One profound transformation would beget another. Along with new societal structures would come an increasing need to abstract: to eliminate the last mimetic traces of nature with an entirely fresh set of cognitive signals. Already, out of the Fertile Crescent in the Near East, the first alphabets would have made their appearance. Soon, even in Provence, the carved sign would be replaced by the written sound. A new order would come into play. The pictograph— resemblant, reflexive, metonymic—would vanish forever.

It's all the more moving, today, to find traces of that lost language and, perhaps, one of its quintessential signs: the vulval imprint of the moon goddess herself. Here, though, in Les Collines de Cordes, that scattered sign lies exposed to vandalism, growing atmospheric pollution, and the increasingly frequent brushfires that have come to ravish the surrounding undergrowth. Reduced today to a *terrain vague*, the area itself has been enclosed in wire fencing by its irate proprietors, but little can be done, ultimately, to protect these rare pictographs from the incursion of squatters, delinquents, or, far worse, the well-informed treasure hunters who come to pillage the hypogea.

We're left, as ever, with what remains. Isn't history, in fact, never more than that which, miraculously enough, *survives history*? The salvaged document? The patiently deciphered tablet? The accidentally uncovered tomb? Yes, we're left, at least here, with the scattered pictographs of a culture that hadn't yet codified its signs into script, hadn't yet "civilized" its divinities by the mediation of abstract signifiers. It still basked in mimetic effigy; with these vulval imprints it still felt itself rung—we may assume—in the matricular outlines of an all-embracing lunar cosmogony. Far more advanced cultures would come, soon enough, to replace it. But it's not altogether certain that this culture and the profound deposits it left within the human psyche could, in fact, be replaced. For at an operative level, there'd be nothing, absolutely nothing, with which to replace it. It constitutes foundation itself.

The Skull with the Seashell Ear 🖝

We're duly forewarned. Culture, in the eyes of archeologists, refers exclusively to material culture: to the little we can glean and, upon gleaning, interpret from those vast, subterranean warehouses of mute artifact. Long since removed from any sociocultural context whatsoever, the artifact, be it bone, flint, or the charred tube of some steatite bead, reaches us bereft of instigating factors— language, gesture, ritual. For all intents and purposes, the artifact reaches us blank. It can, of course, be dated. Thanks to thermoluminescent and radio-carbon analyses, a time frame can usually be established. Furthermore, the artifact itself can be compared, typologically speaking, to other artifacts. One bit of material evidence can be brought to substantiate, to testify for another. The artifact remains, nonetheless, an essentially mute object: a thing in a tax-onomy of things, methodically numbered, classified, relegated. It belongs, ul-timately, to nothing more than inventory itself.

Occasionally, though, an object seems to break free from all such relegation. From the tight circle of so many given, scientific determinants, it will assert itself at a depth, a dimension, entirely its own. Such is the case with a skull discovered in 1955 by archeologists excavating a megalithic chamber tomb at Roque d'Aille in the Var. The skull, unearthed from the lowest and consequently earliest stratigraphic layer, had quite clearly undergone cremation. Exposed to the latent heat of a pyre of less than 500 degrees centigrade, the skull, according to modern analyses, hadn't suffered the cellular decomposition that's invariably brought on by higher temperatures. Calcined, it had done little more than blacken.

But it's not the relatively commonplace discovery of a Neolithic skull, dating from the third millennium B.C., that so astonishes us today. It's not even the fact that the skull, upon examination, turned out to be trepanned. It had been carved open, apparently, with the aid of a rough flint—a primitive crown saw—and the brain had been operated on for an estimated period of three hours. The whole intervention had left a cicatrice nine centimeters long. No, it's neither the black skull nor the jagged scar that runs like some kind of virulent root about one side of the skull plate that so fascinates us today, but the ear, the artificial ear, that once locked into the left side of that hollow, black receptacle. Carved from a seashell, the *spondylus Graederopus*, its artisan had used the shell's thick hinge to replicate the earlobe and its shallow vault to imitate the concavity of the ear's outer whorl. Ironically enough, the external ear is also known, anatomically, as a *concha*.

We're left examining, finally, a delicate prosthesis, one of the earliest artificial members ever discovered. It measures sixty-five by thirty-six millimeters: approximately the measurements of an average human ear. Paleopathologists have determined that the subject of this conchate device was almost certainly a woman, a young woman. Furthermore, these specialists are

Neolithic skull and its prosthetic seashell ear,
found at Roque d'Aille. Photo by the author.

convinced that the woman had not only survived that harrowing "open brain" operation, but had gone on to live for many years, for they've detected on the underside of that artificial organ tiny microscopic traces of patina due, unquestionably, to wear. Was this the result of simple abrasion (the mechanical rub of one surface against another) or the deliberate toying, on the young woman's part, with her curious appendage? Had she fondled its slick underside so often that specialists—peering through electromagnetic microscopes five thousand years later—would pick up traces of the infinitesimal luster left there by the play of her fingertips? By the roll of her thumb and forefinger over its nacreous lip?

Who was she, we might ask ourselves? Given her spectacular attribute, had she enjoyed within her given community a particular status? Was she invested, for instance, with divinatory powers? The ability to *hear* what others couldn't? To decipher, say, the opaque messages emanating out of rock or, even likelier, out of water, that element for which she was so expressly equipped? Yes, a medium of sorts, such as one might encounter in ethnological studies: one, that is, whose very powers had arisen out of some initial impediment.

We know, in fact, so very little. Held to a science that refuses to speculate, to consider any hypotheses whatsoever, we're left, finally, with nothing more than the burnt-out husk of a human skull and its curious, hand-carved appendage. We're left (as we're left all too often) with the illegible relic of some extinct civilization. It's as if a curtain had been resolutely drawn between the known and the unknown, between the material fact and the conditions that once generated that fact. It's as if, on methodology alone, we've been denied access to the immense fields of the possible, the probable—to an intuitive reading of a world that itself was constituted upon an uninterrupted series of intuited postulates.

We go on asking, though, don't we? Go on wondering. Was she tall, handsome? Were her eyes green, black, a deep pellucid blue? More pertinently, did she conceal the iridescent whorl of her artificial ear in a wave of hair or, to the contrary, exhibit it proudly, even vainly, under a high, piled, stick-pinned chignon? What extrasocial functions might she have performed? What shamanistic powers, exercised? Our questions, of course, can only go unanswered. But aren't the questions alone so much richer than the mean trickle of "verifiable fact" that the archeologists have offered us? Might we even come to "cherish the questions themselves," as Rilke once advised his young poet, "like closed rooms, like books written in a very strange tongue"?[1] Might we even begin constituting, indeed, a collection, an entire library of questions? A whole, inexhaustible archive devoted exclusively to wonder, to query, to the unlimited breadth of human speculation? For the curtain that has fallen between the unknown and the known, between the magnitude of our questions and the paucity of our answers, affects not only archeology but every other field of human endeavor as well. As a result, we've grown estranged from origins, deprived of even the vaguest glimpses of those first, founding landscapes. Today, nothing can be acknowledged that hasn't first been processed, electronically channeled, compiled. We're on the far side, now, of inception. It's as if the dark, floating universe from which humankind has always drawn solace and the impalpable reflection of its own deepest identities has entirely vanished.

The issue itself is paramount. Have we been discussing the charred remnants of a prehistoric skull and its auricular prosthesis, or the relics, say, of some Neolithic medium, some priestess both consulted and revered for her extrasensory powers? Have we been discussing, in short, bones, or breath: detrital remainders, or the delicate apparatus of one who might well have been charged with the reception of the weightless, the evanescent, the impalpable? The question alone is well worth asking. It might, in turn, lead us through the drawn curtains themselves. Might bring us onto an ontological level of reasoning in which—at its very limits—we might encounter traces of our own long since absconded identity.

En l'absence de sépultures, la parure est peu connue.
JEAN COURTIN, *LE NÉOLITHIQUE DE LA PROVENCE*

"Now that they accustomed to burn or bury with them, things wherein
they excelled, delighted, or which were dear unto them, either as fare-
wells unto all pleasure, or vain apprehension that they might use them
in the other world, is testified by all Antiquity."
SIR THOMAS BROWNE, "HYDRIOTAPHIA,"
IN *RELIGIO MEDICI AND OTHER WORKS*

West-Southwest

"In the absence of burial sites, little can be said about their self-embellishments,"

writes Jean Courtin, one of Provence's most outstanding archeologists in re-

gard to a particular Neolithic settlement. Burial sites? Self-embellishments? The

two terms seem to clash, one against the other, as totally antithetical. If burials

can only suggest death and bereavement, self-embellishments, to the contrary,

resonate with life, life abundant, luxuriant. How, indeed, did Neolithic societies,

living over four thousand years earlier, reconcile these two terms and, by ex-

tension, the two diametrically opposite conditions of life and death? Existence

and nonexistence? *Eros*, ultimately, and *Thanatos?*

The dead, we learn, were buried with all their finery. Decked in necklaces,

bracelets, and talismans, and accompanied, more often than not, by the tools,

weapons, and ceramics of their day-to-day life, they were dressed for—as if

dispatched toward—a second life. How, though, could this second life have

been very different from the first, given the life-perpetuating characteristics of all that finery? The metonymy of all that artifact? In examining grave goods from this particular period, none can be considered primarily symbolic in its function: none is invested, that is, with transfigurate value. In this transliteration of the identical, soapstone bead equals soapstone bead; a rock crystal pendant, a rock crystal pendant. Here, everything as if celebrates the "same." Everywhere, in fact, in Neolithic burial rites, we discover a marked absence of otherness. This suggests redundancy, replication: a second life identical, in its material aspects, to the first. For these prehistoric people, "life after death," according to the archeologist Gérard Sauzade, "was nothing more in reality than a state of 'survival;' that is to say, a prolongation of life but at a reduced rhythm."[1]

We're dealing here with some of the earliest agrarian communities in western Europe. We may assume that the "psychic structure" of these people was profoundly marked by the mysteries of the vegetal: the stabilized source, now, of their sustenance. Inevitably, this psychic—call it mystico-religious—investment of the grain would affect the very nature of their vision. How could it help but determine the character of their rituals and, most especially, that of their burial rites? Even if the Neolithics weren't the first to inter their dead in a flexed, fetal position—in a posture, that is, of incipient rebirth—they were the first to do so on a regular, collective, institutionalized basis. "Planted," these germinal corpses, these embryos wrapped in all the regalia of an ongoing existence, might well have been expected to "sprout" at the appropriate moment, to "spring" into an afterlife of their own. There, regenerated, they could only resemble their previous selves. Even on the raised octave of an afterlife, "grain" could do little but equal "grain"; the "dried seedlings" of one season, the "shoots" of the next.

We've entered, here, a prehistoric discourse based essentially on reiteration: a vision founded on the recurrent, the cyclical, the fixed rotation of the heavens above, the wheel of the seasons beneath. If, in this discourse, "word" has come to equal "word," we may assume that the conjunction of these words—so equal in weight, density, tenure—could only occur at a propitious distance, one from the other.

⬳

Manifestly, it wasn't for the living that they built colossal structures, but for the dead. Indeed, it's a fair indication to compare the poverty of their dwellings— natural shelters for the most part or provisional *plein air* huts of thatch, hide, or daubed clay—with those megalithic chamber tombs they constructed, at such immense effort, for the deceased. Clearly, they set a far higher value on that discourse—the transliteration of the corpse—than on the grammar of their own fixed existence. We only have to examine the scant traces of their dwellings in relation to their tombs (mistakenly called dolmens in the nineteenth century in a revisionist attempt to Celticize such structures). If the dwellings left little more than potsherds, flint, and the vaguest traces, here and there, of earthworks, the chamber tombs still stand, more often than not, in all their monumental grandeur.

Usually situated in dramatic relief against the side of a hill or upon its summit, these structures seem to draw, to magnetize unto their assembled masses all the chthonic forces of their immediate surroundings. They appear to be collecting, compressing those very forces for the sake of some impending release. Usually paved, invariably pillared with rock uprights called orthostats and capped with table-stones that can weigh up to 180 tons, these burial chambers have far outlasted every other structure of that given period. As often the case with archeological vestige, it is the houses of the dead that finally "speak."

Dolmen du Villard at Lauzet-Ubaye.
Photo courtesy Gérard Sauzade.

Even if many of the tombs themselves have suffered partial or total degradation (converted into shooting blinds or hovels for itinerant shepherds, or simply ransacked by clandestine treasure hunters), enough of them remain relatively intact today, both in terms of their structure and their content, to offer an abundance of information. In Provence these collective sepultures appeared relatively late.[2] As the expression of a rising social hierarchization within Neolithic communities (the dead, presumably, were buried according to caste or clan affiliation), this megalithic movement, originating along the Atlantic coastline, would take two full millennia to reach Provence. There, it would last well over fifteen hundred years, beginning in the late Neolithic (in about 3500 B.C.), vanishing only at the very outset of the Bronze Age. It might be mentioned in passing that we have here a rare instance of prehistoric acculturation traveling in an easterly direction. Invariably, the great routes of cultural penetration would do quite the opposite. As we know, the "Neolithic Revolution," with all its innovating techniques, had infiltrated Europe from east to west, moving either by sea, across the Mediterranean, or by land, following the confluents of the Danube. Curiously enough, it's only in reaching its natural geographic limits along the Atlantic coastline that the first chamber tombs would as if erupt out of the rocky soil of Brittany.

Nothing more fully epitomizes the sedentary nature of Neolithic societies than their chamber tombs. "A people who dig or construct burial vaults," as one archeologist put it, "is no longer nomadic."[3] We're dealing, after all, with agrarian communities that had come to occupy and cultivate delineated areas of earth on a permanent basis for the first time in human existence. We may assume that, within the seasonal round, they constructed their megalithic tombs in winter when their fields lay fallow.[4] Not only would a work force be available at this particular period (as were their Egyptian counterparts, the pyramid builders), but they could benefit from the frozen state of the topsoil in order to slide, on wooden winches most likely, the massive slabs of their ledgers. Even in Provence, ice can cover the ground—in the early hours, at least—for several months of the year.

Capped in round domes, in tumuli of earth and rubble, the rectangular chamber tombs served as collective sepulchers over prolonged periods of time. They often contain the remains of thirty to forty individuals. These remains, however, are rarely in anatomical connection. Displaced, scattered, or crushed under a paving of small cobbles, they've suffered the abuse, or simply the indifference, of so much successive inhumation. Only what lies on the topmost level remains relatively intact.[5] Everywhere, though, intermingled among the bones themselves, one finds beads, amulets, perforated seashells. Spilling, for instance, over a dislocated clavicle will lie a necklace of bright white *Columbella* interspersed with slick, polished cylinders of blue soapstone. Axe heads, arrowheads, flint daggers, not to mention all the ceramic ware offered up as *viatica*, will lie in hopeless disarray about the broken rib cages, shinbones, fibulae of these prehistoric skeletons. Everything but the bones themselves still speaks of dress, preparation. Speaks of the self-embellishments of those setting out—as if celebrant, filled with anticipation—on that ultimate journey.

It should be noted that throughout Provence, Languedoc, and Roussillon, the vestibules or corridors leading past the chamber tombs themselves and toward the exterior world beyond point, infallibly, in a west-southwesterly direction.[6] Most are oriented between 240 and 260 degrees in that direction, both in regard to their floor alignment below and their "axis of visibility" above. This seemingly minor observation is charged with great relevance, for, oriented in that direction, we find ourselves facing the setting sun: the direction, that is, of all solar-funereal mythologies. This setting sun, in Eliade's words, had the power to "inhale the souls of the dead."[7] As psychopomp, the sun drew, guided those souls through the dark reaches of the underworld, only to charge itself with their resuscitation the next morning in its diurnal rebirth. As much hierophant as psychopomp, the sun enjoyed—in the mysteries of its own end-less regeneration—an ambivalent power, reigning over both life and death, radiance and obscurity, the here and hereafter.[8]

West-southwest, indeed. For these megalithic tombs were virtually *pointed*, and the dead they contained virtually dressed: *addressed* in the direction of their rebirth. How close we are to the cyclical mysteries of the grain itself, to both its burial as seed and its germination as seed. Within the context of a Neolithic economy based essentially on the production of cereals, we shouldn't be sur-prised to discover in these rituals an equivalent preoccupation with the recur-rent, the self-replicating. As mentioned previously, the dead were likely to be sent toward an identical, if remote, world of their own. There, they could be expected to reappear in all their finery, equipped, if need be, with the weapons, implements, and ceramics they'd managed to import from their previous lives.

Haven't we, here, an instance of pure translation? Of the word *translation*, that is, in its original (one might even say, veritable) sense, as something *trans-ferred*? A saint's bones, for instance, in Medieval Latin, were "translated" (*trans-latio*) into the bejeweled receptacle of their reliquary. As for ourselves, aren't we continuously translating our own thoughts, our own fears and desires: trans-ferring them from one point, one level of apprehension, to another? Call it music, poetry, prayer. Whatever, it's within our very nature, it would seem, to reiterate experience—but only through the bias of a privileged medium and across a distance (be it intuited, invoked, or simply contemplated) sufficiently removed from our own day-to-day susceptibilities.

Don't we, after all, under certain pressures, motivated by a particular set of circumstances, occasionally face west-southwest ourselves? And, in those chosen moments, haven't we, in the granary of our breath, an address especially intended for such circumstances? There, where "Nimrod is lost in *Orion*, and *Osyris* in the Dogge-starre,"[9] as Sir Thomas Browne put it, don't we ourselves bury our words, our very language, but only for the sake of their eventual resuscitation? That "grain" might equal "grain," but only as a germinated entity: there on the far, the opposite, the facing side, that is, of the intervening night.

A Twilight Industry ⌇

One can still *feel* the marks left by the beating of stone mallets, four thousand years earlier, even if one can't entirely *see* them. Less than a millimeter deep, these dull indentations score the rock face of ledges over an area of several square kilometers in the Monts de Vaucluse. Just detectable at the very tips of one's grazing fingers, they bear witness to the Neolithic industry of flint extraction. Here, nodules of that indispensable mineral were worked free from their limestone matrix. The tiny, barely perceptible blow marks thus created still circumscribe, in vague aureoles, a plethora of gutted cavities. In dull, studded circles, they leave, four millennia later, their ghostly traces.

The site itself was a single, vast, outdoor atelier. It covered an area eight kilometers long and approximately two to three hundred meters wide, following, essentially, the dried-out riverbed of the Vallon des Vergiers in the *commune* of Murs. One can readily imagine, today, the sound that so many countless quartzite mallets must have made, tapping the flint nodules free from their limestone encasements. Imagine groups of Neolithic quarry workers prying loose those obdurate eggs, big as hedgehogs and hard, even harder than tempered steel. Flint constituted, of course, the essential element of Stone Age technology. Curiously enough, however, it was the mallets themselves that first aroused the interest of archeologists. Aroused and perplexed, for the mallets, hewn, rasped, and furrowed with great mastery, appeared to belong to a far more advanced stage of technological development than the chipped flint itself, lying about these abandoned work sites in sizable deposits. Often a meter deep, the deposits contained little more, it seemed, than waste products, the "rejects" of a far less developed industry. If the mallets could be clearly identified as belonging to the end of the late Neolithic (about 2300 B.C.), the flint was originally considered to be Mousterian. The difference, of course, was enormous. The first archeologists, however, had a ready-made answer for such an apparent antinomy. They thought that the site had been continuously occupied over that vast expanse of time and contained, therefore, vestiges of several disparate cultures.

It would take a local aristocrat, Vayson de Pradenne, to dispel this notion altogether and establish the chronological unity of both mallet and flint. Even as a boy he had been fascinated by this open-air atelier which wound, like a river of cracked mineral, through the high, heavily overgrown hills above Murs. Late in the last century, he began mallet hunting with his uncle. At that time, the mallets still lay about the surface of the ground, as if the Neolithic quarry workers themselves had abandoned the site only moments earlier. Carved out of a local rose quartzite, they weighed between two and four kilos and varied in color from salmon pink to brick red. Most were furrowed—grooved—for hafting. Together, Pradenne and his uncle would collect these mallets in deep straw baskets. Whenever their baskets grew too heavy, they'd stash their "treasures" away in the thick, prickly undergrowth of a juniper bush.

Pradenne would go on exploring and collecting specimens from this site throughout the better part of his life.[1] Furthermore, he'd continue reading and interpreting his discoveries in the light of archeology's rapidly evolving methodology. It wasn't until 1931, however, that, fearing his own impending death, he decided to publish all the data and documentation that he'd amassed on the site itself. Fruit of a lifetime's devotion, "L'industrie des ateliers à maillets de Murs"[2] is an eloquent testimony to that river of cracked mineral. In this thirty-three-page report, Pradenne would put forth conclusive evidence regarding the contemporaneity of the site itself. The entire atelier, he proposed, belonged to a single specific moment in prehistory: namely, the extreme end of the Neolithic. He substantiated his argument with the following observations:

First, the quantity of mineral waste at each particular worksite was directly proportionate to the number of mallets found. The higher the pile of knapped flint and chipped limestone, the greater the likelihood of discovering several of those stout, Neolithic hammerheads. Flint and mallet, he soon came to realize, were inseparably related. Second, the flint, often lying in heaps over a meter deep, displayed the exact same facture throughout, clearly indicating its chronological unity. Within those heaps, Pradenne would uncover his mallets. He even managed to discern, in the near-microscopic pits of their striking face, traces of the very flint they'd been called upon to extract four thousand years earlier.

On evidence alone, he came to some stunning conclusions. In exploring, year after year, all eight kilometers of that ongoing worksite, he had become a witness to a culture, an entire civilization, in full decline. Nothing illustrated that decline more fully than the manner in which these late Neolithics treated their raw materials. Indeed, in reading Pradenne's essay today, one can't help but think of another culture in full decline—our own—which has utilized its natural resources and manufactured its finished goods in very much the same manner. Here, briefly, are several of the astounding conclusions Pradenne drew from a lifetime's observations:

These late Neolithic craftsmen, in exploiting an ever-expanding area of ground in response to an ever-increasing demand, had moved, ipso facto, from an artisanal work ethic to an industrial one.

In so doing, their field of vision had gone from a fixation on the specific (and thus, the precise, the meticulously executed) to an expanding preoccupation with the general, the mass-produced.

This expansion in space generated the conditions for an accelerated attitude toward time: the clearly rushed, clearly negligent execution evident in the better part of the artifacts themselves (which caused the first archeologists to mistake this industry for that of the Mousterian) testifies to this very acceleration.

Working at an increased pace over an expanding area, the workers themselves couldn't help but squander, in their haste, a greater and greater quantity of raw materials (thus the huge piles of chipped flint, still evident today).

Given the abundance of this squander and the poor quality of whatever worked flint still remains, the finished products of this industry weren't destined for local use but, to the contrary, were "for export only."

The flint, as a prime substance, might have already fallen into a certain discredit with the arrival, at about this time, of the first imported tools fashioned out of an entirely new substance: bronze.

In reading this somber report, we're likely to find many similarities with our own "postindustrial age": these two perfectly disparate moments in material culture share many characteristics. Point after point, we can trace the all-too-familiar spread and acceleration of human productivity; the resultant squander of natural resources; the primacy given, everywhere, to quantity over quality; the virtual disappearance of all traditional concerns for the meticulously crafted artifact in favor of an increasingly diffuse, "globally oriented" market commodity. In point after point, we're likely to find astonishing echoes in this particular instance of late Neolithic material culture.

Of all those echoes, none, perhaps, is more evocative of our own specific moment in history than the very last: how one prime substance will fall into immediate disfavor with the arrival of another; how flint, quite suddenly, suffered the indifference it did with the introduction of bronze. Today, we are all too familiar with obsolescent materials, with the penultimate moment in any number of derelict industries. Haven't we watched (as one example among many) the total transformation of the printed word in the past few years? Seen it "migrate" from the page to the screen, followed its peregrination from richly inked, deeply embedded, machine-struck pages to the flickering, green ephemera of electronic data. Here, we're the witnesses of a massive breakdown in this most fundamental cultural constant. From typeset to printout, we've watched the word, in its *residency* as word, as if volatilize.

We live as a society at the very edge of our own innovated world, looking backward. Fortunately, there are other edges, other precipitous moments, that we discover as we search history and prehistory for precedents. Here, for instance, in the Vallon des Vergiers that Pradenne explored throughout his life, haven't we found, in fact, a perfect corollary? Here, among the rubble, among the rejected flint of a twilight industry, lies a point of fracture, a moment of pure cleavage, remarkably similar to our own.

This morning, I went on inspecting those dull little blow marks, what the mallets left, pocking the limestone's face, nearly four thousand years earlier. I went on reading those minuscule indentations at the tips of my fingers like some otherwise indecipherable script. It's late spring. Broom, all about, squirts lemon yellow from the extremity of its long, strawlike shoots. Above me, cicadas have already set up station. Their dry, monotonous vibrato seems to sizzle, louder and louder, as the temperature rises. As for myself, my fingertips go on moving from one eloquent little hollow to another. From one scarcely perceptible cavity to the next. No matter how ephemeral, vestige—one comes to learn—can teach us everything we need to know, and knowing, anticipate.

in memory of Sylvain Gagnière, dean of Provençal archeologists

Stelae 🖋

THE EMERGENCE OF HUMAN FIGURATION

Surrounded today in self-image, we readily forget how slowly we first came to represent our own features, to give some kind of graphic form to our own physical presence. Indeed, in the immensely long history of prehistoric figuration, we're the last "subject" to emerge. We come, it might be said, to complete the bestiary. Carved into limestone, rounded out of clay, or simply scratched across the slate surface of some talismanic plaque, the human face arrives, finally, as a kind of belated gesture: a conclusive act.

Yes, slowly, hesitatingly, we come to depict ourselves. We enter the mirror of our own self-realization almost despite ourselves: despite, that is, some deeply hidden, atavistic reserve. That face, at first, for all its human attributes, doesn't depict an individual so much as a spirit, a demiurge, an entity endowed with certain human features but placed in a context that remains essentially "dehumanized." In Provence, for instance, the first faces—the first anthropomorphic figurations, that is—represent tutelary spirits. Associated with necropolises, they were charged, we can only assume, with the transmutation of the souls of the dead. Carved on flat, limestone slabs, these late Neolithic funerary figures belonged to a world of shadows, to that flickering space in which the dead themselves transited: that dark, transparent interstice between the here and the hereafter.

Discovered usually quite by chance, these stelae have been unearthed over the years by farmers during their deep winter plowings or uncovered by masons while restoring, say, a crumbling drystone wall. Often, grave goods dating from the same period (2400–2200 B.C.) have been discovered within the immediate area, confirming the relation of these early anthropomorphic artifacts with funerary rites. Even more determinate, bits of terra-cotta coffers for housing cinerary remains have been discovered near Trets in the Var within the same archeological milieu as fragments from fifteen individual stelae. Everywhere throughout the Mediterranean basin, idols, statuettes, statue menhirs, and slabs such as these, dating from the same period, have been discovered in (or in the immediate area of) burial pits, collective tombs, crematoria. What in each case we're witnessing here—from the Cyclades in the Aegean to Galicia on the Iberian Peninsula—is the birth, within a sepulchral context, of human figuration. We'd at last come to fashion our very likeness.

More than any other feature, it's the abundant head of hair, executed in champlevé, that distinguishes the first Provençal stelae (*les stèles à chevrons*). The geometric patterns employed in the representation of this feature—lozenge, herringbone, zigzag—have often been compared to stellar configurations. The hair seems to ripple in a thick, wickerlike weave of constellated points. Some prehistorians, however, have interpreted these motifs as aquatic, as that of running or tumbling water. One interpretation, of course, needn't exclude another. Hair, star, and water: the human, the stellar, and the aquatic might readily co-

*Late Neolithic funerary stele from Lauris-
Puyvert. Photo courtesy Musée Calvet, Avignon.*

exist within the same symbolic field as representative of three simultaneous levels of apprehension.

There is one argument, however, that would tend to favor an aquatic interpretation. This particular civilization (distantly related to the lake-dwelling Lagozzian in northern Italy) invariably inhabited sites within easy reach of running water. The sites themselves, usually situated on hillocks, all overlook rivers. We may assume that these people had been driven down out of the surrounding plateaus for any number of reasons: a severe climate, prevalent everywhere in the western Mediterranean at that time, would have caused drought and penury; massive campaigns of deforestation for the sake of clearing pastureland would have created, in turn, land erosion; and the abusive practice of denshiring would have resulted in an even greater exhaustion of the topsoil. These people, living as they did near riverbeds in the latter half of the third millennium B.C., undoubtedly supplemented their diet with trout, salmon, and crayfish. The waters just beneath and the star-studded heavens just above might well have been emblematic, in their eyes, of existence itself. Significantly enough, these first, emergent portraits were endowed with a rich cosmological decor, redolent of the natural world that surrounded their scattered riverine settlements.

We have, then, human figuration: the inaugural appearance, in this particular part of the Neolithic world, of a face, despite a high level of stylization. Framed within that abundant head of hair, we find (in most cases) a rectangle in which a pair of eyes and a nose have been carved in relief. The nose and the closely abutting pair of eyes have often been interpreted as representing the male genitals; below, at the base of the empty rectangle (clearly suggesting the face itself), a narrow passage, that of the neck, has often been read as representing the vagina. Here again, we're not obliged to choose between diverse interpretations. At separate levels, they might readily coexist, one superimposed upon the other. Subliminally, the genitalia might well lie, graphically coded, beneath the apparent figuration of the face itself.

More than any other feature depicted on these Provençal stelae, however, it's the mouth or, rather, the *absence* of mouth, that has drawn scholars' attention. "Throughout all of Mediterranean Europe," writes André d'Anna, "these anthropomorphic representations are characterized by that same, somewhat puzzling omission."[1] We mustn't forget that we've entered, here, a world of shadows, a netherworld in which the dead, freshly interred, had already begun evolving toward an afterlife. Death, of course, is silent. And these tutelary figures, charged as they were with the transmutation of souls, represented passage: an intermediary zone between the realm of the deceased and that of the resuscitated. As such, they're portrayed mute. What's more, as d'Anna points out, they're portrayed deaf: they're not only devoid of mouths, but ears. Linguistically speaking, we've entered a kind of suspended hiatus between one "language" and another, one "existence" and the next. The absence of speech, however, doesn't exclude that of sight, for these guardian spirits seem to gaze from their flat limestone slabs with astonishing intensity. By their gaze alone, they seem endowed with the power to induce, conduct, deliver. We might even speculate that we've entered (at least within the transitory context of that muffled decor) a level of metaphysical apprehension monopolized by sight and sight alone. Here, it's the gaze—attentive, anticipatory—that's charged, it would seem, with all cognition.

It's no mere coincidence that these first figurative representations happen to depict anthropomorphic spirits rather than individuals proper. Hovering in that half-world between the here and the hereafter—between, that is, the human and the divine—they're the first manifestations of an emergent religiosity. Everywhere, now, throughout the Neolithic world, an entirely new conception of existence had come into play. At no other moment, perhaps, in the history of consciousness would humankind undergo such a sense of rupture with its own past and such a need to reevaluate itself in the light of so many fresh determinants. What, indeed, *did* happen at that very moment? What essentially was the cause for such an absolute cleavage in human consciousness? That "moment" varies according to the region involved, according to the slow but inexorable sweep westward of the Neolithic Revolution. If, however, that "moment" varies in time according to the area in question, typologically it remains identical. For it occurs whenever a given society moves from predation to production, from an economy based on hunting and gathering to one of farming and stockbreeding. The "moment," then, is that pivotal instant in which humankind, dependent from its very origin on the bounty of nature, discovers the means by which it can determine—within the given limits of soil, climate, and its first rudimentary agrarian techniques—the production of its own food supply. This represents, of course, an immense triumph over the precarious conditions under which humankind had always sought to sustain itself. It also happens to mark, however, an absolute severance with the past. We'd now come to plant, tend, and harvest what we had always been given; come to wrest from nature what nature had always provided. Within the tight weave of an ecological fabric, a rent suddenly appears. Between humankind and nature, a sense of rupture, removal, separation replaces that of an essential, deep-seated unity. In coming into our own as food producers, we'd have quite unwittingly "broken contract." That sense of rupture, of ever-increasing removal, would have an all-determinate effect on our psychic structure. In considering ourselves, now, as separable and separate entities, we'd have entered, in Hegelian terms, a state of "self-consciousness." We'd have begun seeing ourselves, that is, as something *other than* and *different from* creatures belonging to a single, inextricable creation. In short, in coming to control our own food supply, we'd have acquired a *separate status*.

Ineluctably, a sense of alienation would arise out of that instigating "moment," that act of primal violation. On a mythological level, it would find expression (at a somewhat later date) in Prometheus's theft of the thunderbolt from the gods overhead, and—in its Judeo-Christian counterpart—Adam's theft of the forbidden apple from the garden. In each case, disgrace, humiliation, would be the price exacted, what humankind would have to pay for having "seized control."

Recognizing ourselves as separate entities, as if extracted from the matrix of that aboriginal unity, we'd begin seeing ourselves, portraying ourselves, as discrete creatures. In that ever-growing "self-consciousness," we'd begin carving our first deliberately figurative, anthropomorphic representations. At the very outset, however, it isn't ourselves we portray but, as already mentioned, those guardians, those figures stationed halfway between the human and the divine. One might even say, at this particular stage, that the separation between the two hadn't yet been totally consummated, that the "moment" is slow in realizing itself, that the initial matrix is reluctant to divide. Indeed, the history, the prehistory, of human consciousness and its subsequent manifestations as art over the next millennia would be increasingly dominated by that division. For at the very same time that we would come to recognize ourselves— *realize* ourselves—as separate entities, we would come to project our first divinities. One evinces the other. Self-realization, admitting as it does to difference, separation and, ultimately, loss, produces—in compensation—its estranged counterpart in the form of gods, divine projections. We cannot see and depict *who we are*, finally, without seeing and depicting *who we aren't*. "A vertical topology begins to develop at the heart of the human psyche," writes Jacques Cauvin, "in which an initial state of anguish finally dissipates, but only at the price of an intense mental effort in an ascensional direction. That effort is experienced as an appeal to a divine instance that is both beyond and above humankind itself."[2]

It would go well past the limited ambitions of this essay to trace the iconographic development of figuration as it divides, at this point, into those two increasingly distinct domains. Suffice to say that that development, beginning with so many anonymous, highly stylized funerary markers throughout the entire Mediterranean basin, would grow increasingly individuated, self-personifying, in the effigiation of both the human and the divine. One, indeed, would mirror the other: face and its inaccessible counterface; flesh and the hallucinatory canonization of spirit; humankind, in short, and its divinities. Irresoluble, the twin character of this dialectic would come to express, in Cauvin's words, "the anthropological effects of a deep-seated *malaise*."[3]

For the moment, however, we're still at the very outset of human representation. With these early Provençal stelae, we're witnesses to nothing more or less than that auroral moment in human consciousness in which we first came to see ourselves as something separable, something other, something different from the creatures of an indissoluble creation. Slowly, hesitatingly, we would come to mime our own physiognomy in these mute and, as yet, asexual (or simply androgynous) figurations. At the same time, we'd have begun hoeing the earth, harvesting its grain, and stocking its produce in ceramic receptacles: taking, in short, the first decisive steps toward the eventual control of our natural milieu. We would never stop, either. The history of humanity (as, alas, we well know) would be the history of that domination on an ever-accelerating scale. Spreading our control over all living matter, we'd come to discover the secret source of energy itself, hidden at the very heart of the seemingly inviolable molecule. Concurrently, portraiture would assume (at least in certain quarters) hyperrealistic proportions.

Slowly, hesitatingly, we would come to recognize ourselves, reflected in these very first mirrors of self-realization. Here in Provence, toward the end of the third millennium B.C., these anthropomorphic figurations bear witness to that moment, that passage leading to self-awareness. With them, we'd come to admit to our freshly acquired status as separate entities in the midst of a hitherto inseparable ensemble, a naturally constituted unity. Despite that deep, atavistic reserve, we'd slowly but inexorably enter that exile we'd come to call selfhood, individuation. Almost despite ourselves, we'd acquire, finally, our isolated identities.

for Hugues Bonnetain

PART II

Bronze, and Soon After, Iron ❧

On a Bronze Age Earring 🖋

It must have come up with autumn's knee-deep plowings and laid there throughout the winter: a tiny artifact in a throw of scooped mud. Acid green, it looked more like glass, at first: the lip, say, of some narrow medieval vial. In the palm of my hand, however, the weight of this chance discovery indicated metal. Indicated bronze. A thin sliver no more than two centimeters wide, it was shaped in the form of a tapering crescent. Moon, I thought. I was holding in the palm of my hand a hand-pounded, protohistoric lunar slip: a bit of bronze that had been worked—in the first centuries, no doubt, of metallurgy—into a dangling, little ornament.

There's a thrill, of course, to such finds: an instant in which one is struck by the miracle of so much sheer fortuity. How does something so small, so inconspicuous, survive not merely an endless succession of heavy, mechanical plowings but three thousand consecutive years of ignorance, indifference, drift? One can only wonder. Wonder and marvel all the more at the complexity of circumstances that brought this minute object, finally, to one's focused attention. So much ocean, I kept thinking, for the sake of such a tiny, salvaged scrap.

My first reaction—one of simple astonishment—gave way, however, to something far deeper. For the object of my attention—still lying in the palm of my hand—turned, bit by bit, to a subject. More than merely "something," it revealed itself as the last distinguishing trace of some long-since vanished "someone," a sole, surviving vestige. As an accessory, it might well have constituted—who knows?—a cherished part of that "someone's" self-image. Might well have been the bauble by which she chose, in intimate moments, to recognize herself in the midst of an arduous life. I could only speculate. How, in fact, can one respond to "someone" who isn't? Voice without sound, language without words, this lunar droplet, nonetheless, begged to be heard. I could only listen. Could only assume, under the circumstances, my role as witness.

Aren't we always, indeed, witnesses to artifact, to the muffled discourse of the inanimate, to the irresonant world of vestige? Aren't we always, in fact, called to testify for those who can't? Because the dead, we realize, have only ourselves; by the bias of relic, only the gloss of our own passing testimonials. In the archeological order of things, don't the dead—out of those heavy, earth-choked layers—continually solicit our attention? Isn't it we that they invariably delegate? Verbally invest? We who live, if only momentarily, on that ultimate stratum: one of air, wind, unbroken weather?

I imagined her blonde. I imagined her long, straightforward features and the rather surprising length of her body, wrapped to the ankles in roebuck. I imagined, as well, a certain weight to her gaze, the heavy domes of her eyelids. Children, I wondered, lost in childbirth? The prevalence, everywhere, of early death? The foreshadowing, perhaps, of her own? Here, one needn't imagine what has already been determined: life expectancy in the Bronze Age was exceedingly low. I followed her, that very moment, as she turned. Saw her stand, now, in profile, her fingers forking through the thick tuft of her honey blonde hair, piling it high as she did. And, in that very same second, I saw it. Saw it glint, not acid green, but gold. Saw that small lunar trinket quiver, dangling from her now uncovered earlobe like some minuscule spoon bait.

It was nothing more, of course, than image, than an imaginary reconstitution of a stray object. Yes, so much imagery, couched in the weights and measures of an equally evanescent medium, that of language itself. But between them, between the words of the living and the intimations of the dead— between, that is, the spoken and the bespoken—hadn't a glint actually broken through? Wedged, impacted between two distinct realms, hadn't a ray—a pure emanation— escaped? In the palm of one's hand, come to radiate?

for Odile and Jean Taffanel

Echoes in Clay ⟐

Jubilation—that rare word—comes immediately to mind. For the tiny, incised figures that adorn the flanks of these late Bronze Age ceramics—their arms raised skyward or hand-in-hand linked like dancers in the round—seem to be celebrating some kind of joyous rite. They're not alone, either. Running about the contours of these hand-coiled ceramic bowls in so many unbroken processionals come horses, the crosslike spokes of carts, *charrettes*. All of these figures, be they the celebrants themselves, their horses and carts, or the full cortege of stylized motifs that accompany them (triangles, triglyphs, zigzags, checkerboards, an endless variation on the meander or fret-pattern), yes, all of these figures seemed marked by a rigorous suppression of the curve, the curvilinear. In these depicted celebrations, everything meets at sharp angles, defines itself in the crisp geometry of an emergent script. In examining these pictographs, we have the distinct impression of observing the birth (or, at least, the first stirrings) of some incipient written language. Of, indeed, writing itself.

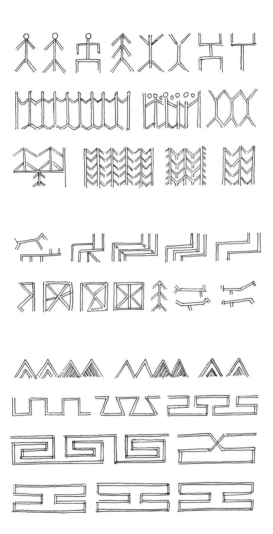

*Anthropomorphic, zoomorphic, and geometric
motifs recurrent in Mailhacien pottery. Drawing
by Gabriel Sobin.*

Before taking a closer look at these imminently semiotic units, we might ask who these people were and what, exactly, they might have been celebrating. The culture itself, known as Mailhacien, draws its name from the protohistoric site of Le Cayla-de-Mailhac, situated twenty-five kilometers north of Narbonne in the first, rippling, vineyard-covered folds of the Minervois. The eponym, in turn, has come to apply to an entire ethnic substratum, relatively limited in time (870–700 B.C.) and essentially littoral in space: it inhabited, in small, scattered, agrarian communities, an area extending from the valley of the Aude to that of the Rhone. Mediterranean in character and probably north Italian (Ligurian) in origin, these people developed, nonetheless, a thoroughly original culture of their own. Indeed, their ceramic ware attests to that originality. Joyous in expression, in its continually generative decor, it clearly celebrates an age of abundance, security, well-being. Moreover, the processionals that circumscribe one earthenware vessel after another suggest, in so many eloquent pictographs, pilgrims in the very act of expressing thanks for that evident state of plenitude.

Where were they traveling? For certainly, these Mailhaciens were traveling "somewhere," given the fact that they're nearly always depicted in groups, accompanied on either side by so many stylized quadrupeds (horses if not oxen) and the cruciform spokes of so many suggested carriages. Each of these ensembles expresses movement, displacement, if not some ceremonial form of pilgrimage itself. Michel Py, the eminent protohistorian, has suggested that these agropastoral communities might, in fact, have been "pastoro-agrarian": predominantly herdsmen, that is.[1] As such, they might well have practiced some form of seasonal migration, bringing their livestock down to the coastal plains in the winter months (several archeological excavations along the Languedoc coastline attest to such seasonal occupation in the late Bronze Age) before returning, each spring, to their perched villages in the *garigues*, or hinterlands, above. Such a transhumant practice is, in fact, more than likely, and it might well explain the subject matter of many, if not most, of their incised pictographs.

We need only look at the seasonal migration of Papago Indians in southern Arizona to discover a somewhat similar practice. There, until recently, the Papagos would travel considerable distances on horseback or in horse-driven conveyances to harvest the ripe fruit of the saguaro cactus. Immediately after those harvests, the entire tribe would celebrate, in situ, the bounty of a desert that each spring unfailingly offered its wild succulents. Might we be examining, in these protohistoric pictographs, the expression of similar festive celebrations? Or, on a scale far more extensive in both space and time, might they represent the iconographic shorthand of communities that divided the year between two separate homelands, practicing two separate economies (in this instance, farming and stockbreeding), each of which fell, presumably, under the auspices of an opposite, if complementary chieftain? Called "moiety societies" by anthropologists, they'd have had good reason to celebrate their biannual homecomings, not to mention the cyclical mysteries of so much natural abundance.

Indeed, there are indices within the pictographs themselves to support such a hypothesis, for everything in this emergent script resonates with marked duality. The very incisions with which the pictographs were drawn in the fresh, unfired clay happen to be *twin* incisions. Executed in a series of single rectilinear strokes, the pictograms—we may assume—were drawn with a forked instrument: an awl, most likely, carved out of bone, wood, or possibly feather, and cleaved, at its extremity, into two identical tines. Every stroke is accompanied, therefore, by its complement. Each echoes its reiterative "other."

*A Mailhacien potsherd with characteristic twin
incisions. Drawing by the author.*

We're given, in so much running ideography, the vision of a world in a continuous state of self-duplication.

Until now, these twin incisions have been considered as little more than a
graphic device for enhancing the visual effect (*"l'effet décoratif"*) of the pictographs themselves. Enhance them, they certainly do. But might they not, at
the same time, be the expression of something far deeper, of that very self-
duplication itself? Call it, if one will, the graphically coded semiotics of a people who experienced, interpreted, and expressed the world about them in echo-
ing sets of images. In this ongoing grammar of signs, each set of images would
seem to reverberate with an innate sense of the binary.

There's yet another characteristic in the incised Mailhacien ceramic that supports this supposition. The pictographs themselves were painted with one of
two colors once the earthenware vessel itself had been fully fired. The two colors, red and white (ground ocher and crushed calcined bone), possess a signifying value of their own that far exceeds that of the "simply decorative." For
red, in Mailhacien ceramics, invariably indicates a subject that is male or male
associated, and white, female or female associated. Granted, many of the an-

thropomorphic and zoological motifs might be encrusted interchangeably with either one color or the other. This not only underlines the inveterate need of these people to express themselves in dialectical terms but the possibility (given that neither of these two colors predominate) that this was a society that enjoyed a certain measure of sexual equality. One gender is quite free to fulfill the roles of another. We have, however, certain motifs such as the triangle (emblematic, quite possibly, of the flared skirt) that are encrusted exclusively with white pigment. White, too, seems to predominate among the excavated grave goods in female sepulchers, especially in regard to the frequently discovered deposits of blanched scallop shells. These have been unearthed (together with other offerings) only in the immediate vicinity of female cinerary urns.

In a society so prone to codify and—in codifying—to endow each of its signs with its own countersign, it's little wonder that these people were well on their way to creating, as an ultimate codification, a written language of their own. Their pictographs, "the bearer of messages," as Py has qualified them,[2] may be seen as phrases, wrapped sequentially about each incised vessel. They contain meaning even if much of that meaning escapes us today. As to their faultlessly linear, strokelike execution, this can only be interpreted as a deliberate attempt on the part of this late Bronze Age culture to rationalize the curvilinear script of nature itself, thus translating hills, clouds, and anatomical outline into a closed system of dashes, angles, and squares. These people were well on their way, now, to the creation of a parallel script: written language itself. According to Alain Mendoza, one can begin to detect letters in that profusion of pictographs that prefigure the *be* and the *co* of the Iberian alphabet and the *alpha, beta*, etc., of the Greek, several centuries later. Yes, already, according to Mendoza, we can speak of a script bordering on the "*alphabétiforme.*"[3]

What happened, then, to this profoundly evolutionary movement in cultural history? According to Odile and Jean Taffanel—who first discovered the site of Le Cayla-de-Mailhac and its adjacent necropolises over sixty-five years ago and who have spent the intervening years excavating its rich vestigial deposits—the site was invaded, occupied, and annexed by an entirely new civilization at the end of the eighth century B.C. More than merely introducing an alien social culture, these people brought with them a revolutionary technology based on the extraction, manufacture, and diffusion of iron, a harder, more resistant metal than bronze. Even if we admit, today, that this crucial moment of transition from bronze to iron (and consequently from the Bronze Age to the Iron Age) might have been more gradual and assimilative than originally estimated, we still have evidence of a spectacular transformative process within a relatively short period of time. Within that period, an entirely new social structure based on the division of labor and the hierarchization of class would lead, in less than a century, to a warrior elite presiding over an ever widening territory of market-oriented exchange.

For our purposes, we only need consider the ceramic ware itself as exemplary of those massive transformations. The delicately traced, doubly incised Mailhacien pottery disappears altogether with the arrival of these earliest Iron Age societies. It is replaced almost immediately by a series of larger, far less refined earthenware vessels decorated with bold geometric motifs. These motifs were obtained by excision: by the removal, that is, of clay for the sake of a particular stylized effect. More significant, it no longer bore any message whatsoever. Its decor does nothing but decorate. Indeed, the difference in approach, style, and execution between these two cultural vectors couldn't be more absolute. Gone, now, that ideogrammatic script that begs to be written. Begs to be read. Gone, those dancers, those celebrants in one jubilant gathering after another. Gone, the horses, wheels, carts of their collective processionals. These late Bronze Age people, living as they did in small autarkic communities and imbued—given the ideology apparent in their incised pottery—with a deep-seated sense of social equality, possessed a level of culture *intrinsically predisposed to transmission*. Within that world of theirs, every "signifier" seems to have elicited its equivalent "signified," every point, its perfectly matched counterpoint. Within the running script of their pictographs, each element seems to enter, ineluctably, a tightly woven system of reciprocities. In examining this ceramic ware nearly three millennia after its fabrication, we become witnesses, in effect, to a short-lived moment of social, cultural, and spiritual equanimity. In the very twilight of the late Bronze Age, we catch glimpses of an all-too-fleeting period of human plenitude.

Granted, iron would provide societies everywhere, now, with a metal far more effective and dependable than the bronze it had come to replace. An entirely new level of material development had suddenly become possible. Taking every form from the warrior's sword to the peasant's sickle, iron would virtually flood the rapidly evolving protohistoric world in a surprisingly short period of time. Altogether, the Iron Age would mark an irrepressible rise in human technological development. And, concurrently, this technological development would determine the life of societies as rarely before.

It would be fallacious, however, to equate technological development with human advancement. They're all too often, alas, antithetic. We only need consider our own age. In a strict interpretation of the term, the Iron Age (as the last of three periods—Stone, Bronze, and Iron—in the "Three Age System" coined by Christian Thomsen in 1819) doesn't end, in fact, until the explosion of the first atomic bomb over New Mexico in 1944. That age, the Atomic Age, is, of course, our own. Of the unlimited powers we've allowed *technē* to assume over its very subjects (to wit, humanity itself) there's painfully little any of us would say in its defense. We have entered an age that has the technological means to annihilate all creation at any given instant. And, having entered the troubled consciousness of that age, we have begun looking backward. It's not the dancers, the celebrants, or the pilgrims that we're looking back toward, though, but ourselves. It's not the particularities of an ideogrammatic script running around the rim of a late Bronze Age ceramic that we seek to interpret, but the traces of our own inherent tendency to assemble—in so many matching, reflexive units—all the elements of a fully articulated existence. In a "tightly woven system of reciprocities," we have come to investigate our own capacity to give expression to an underlying sense of life-oriented, life-perpetuating determinants.

In reading vestiges such as these, interpreting their tenuous messages, we might, occasionally, uncover a long lost ontology of our own. This, at least, is what the potsherds would seem to suggest.

Baby Burials 🦅

DOMESTIC INHUMATION IN THE IRON AGE

For the archeologist, the past—no matter how remote—has always laid at the tip of some glittering surgical instrument. Sifting meticulously through so much apparent detritus, the field worker—in selecting this, eliminating that—has traditionally given priority to any vestige that might possibly indicate chronology: any deposit, that is, that serves to situate the culture in question within the established sequence of history itself. In so doing, many minute, seemingly inconsequential osteological remains have gone, until fairly recently, overlooked. Too slight, too ephemeral to merit attention, to fit into any rigid classification, the tiny bones of babies—often buried at birth—have been swept aside in favor of materials more readily identifiable. This has been the case, for instance, in Languedoc. There, perinatal remains have been discovered—and, all too often, rejected—buried beneath the mud floors of protohistoric dwellings or in immediately adjacent courtyards.

Only in the last few decades have these burials—labeled by the archeologists as domestic inhumations—come to receive the attention they deserve. Today, in fact, each minuscule collarbone, each shoulder blade (no wider, often, than a periwinkle), the seedling of each incisor still locked within the slender husk of its jawbone, undergoes painstaking scrutiny both in the field and in specially equipped laboratories. In the field, dental and ophthalmological surgical instruments are employed, as is a microvacuum for eliminating extraneous matter in the near-infinitesimal sweep of its two-centimeter nozzle. In the laboratory, osteopathological examinations of those perinatal remains allow archeologists to determine the age of the subject by its teeth (degree of calcification), its skull (level of ossification of the cranial plates) and, of course, by its stature, no matter how minute. As to its sex, this has often been calculated (but with less certainty) by osteometric measurements of both the hip bone and the sciatic notch.

What, though, have all these immensely sophisticated analyses come to tell us in regard to this obscure Iron Age practice itself? Even after we've learned that the youngest subject yet identified happens to be a fetus of seven lunar (six calendar) months (judging by its sole remaining vestige: a femur no wider than a nail clipping), that most of the subjects were stillborn or died within days of their birth, and that none lived for more than a month, we're left wondering. What, in fact, did this practice represent? Attest to? Given that the defunct in these protohistoric communities were invariably buried in necropolises entirely separate from the habitats themselves, the fetus, the stillborn, and the dead nursling were clearly subject to a status of their own. But which? And what, exactly, can these domestic inhumations tell us of a practice that has left traces so tenuous that they could easily be blown away like straw with the least gust of wind?

Buried in pits that average twenty centimeters in depth, these tiny corpses were usually laid on one side or another in a wrapped fetal position, their knees brought level with their chin. Their spinal columns came to describe, thus, a three-quarter circle: a near self-enveloping ellipse. Discovered occasionally intact—in anatomical connection, that is—these human vestiges seem to have undergone no ritual whatsoever at the time of inhumation. Even if the cheek of one stillborn baby has been discovered lying against a tiny collection of pebbles, and that of another cradled in the minuscule cup of one of its hands, none of the usual grave goods—victuals, *viatica*, offerings— have been detected at any of the excavated sites. To the contrary, the pit graves themselves seem to have been covered over as quickly and as unceremoniously as possible with whatever soil happened to be at hand. Often ashen, bearing broken ceramics and the refuse of some adjacent hearth— calcined animal bone, seed, vegetal fiber, etc.—absolutely nothing distinguishes this soil from that of the beaten earth of the surrounding habitat. Furthermore, no stele, no commemorative marker has been found on the surface of any of these earthen floors to indicate the presence, just beneath, of these infant deposits.

What can we assume or simply deduce, then, from all the data accumulated on this particular practice, so prevalent in Languedoc throughout that period (the seventh to the first century B.C.)? Quite clearly, we can dismiss, first of all, three hypotheses that have been advanced over the years. Two of them suggest infanticide: one for the sake of birth control, the other for that of sacrificial offering. We must remember in regard to the suppression of newborns and nurslings (not to mention fetuses) that natural infant mortality in the Iron Age was exceedingly high. There would have been little or no reason to add to that death toll by deliberate suppressions. As for the idea that female births were subject to a certain form of selection (as they'd been, traditionally, in China, for instance) gender determination by osteological examination has done nothing but disprove such a hypothesis.

In regard to ritual sacrifice, once again material evidence has come to dismiss such a notion altogether. If, for instance, at La Escudilla near Castellón de la Plana in the region of Valencia, irrefutable proof of infant sacrifice in the fourth century B.C. has been unearthed (presumably for the sake of assuring—by propitiation—abundant crops and the fecundity of livestock), none of the paraphernalia associated with such a ritual has come to light in Languedoc. At La Escudilla, for example, perinatal remains were buried in terra-cotta urns as opposed to earthen pits. Furthermore, they were accompanied by votive offerings and marked by stone commemorative slabs. None of those indices is present in Languedoc. To the contrary, infant burial in these parts seems characterized by a distinct and sustained absence of any "sign" whatsoever. By a deliberate anonymity.

Drawing on ethnological studies, some archeologists have suggested that these infant deaths—natural in themselves—might have been considered, within Iron Age communities, as "bad deaths." As such, they might not have been deemed worthy of ritual: the purifying rites, that is, of a funeral ceremony. They might well have been destined to "disappear forever, be refused any access to the 'beyond,' find themselves committed, thus, to an irreversible state of non-being."[1] Under such conditions, their tiny bodies would be "buried with little or no ritual whatsoever or simply abandoned—flung—to the elements themselves."[2]

Why, then, were these flexed little corpses—often not much larger than a rabbit—interred within or immediately alongside the family dwelling itself? As if associated as closely—intimately—as possible to the material life of that dwelling: to its voices, smells, its living effusions? As if deposited, secreted in the midst, in the very *locus* of so much ongoing existence?

"The roots of such a tradition," Bernard Dedet has suggested, "may reach deeply into the regional past."³ Indeed, there are precedents for such a tradition in both Languedoc and Provence. Already, in the late Neolithic, traces of infant burial have been detected within inhabited grottoes as opposed, say, to outlying tumuli: the "instinct" for such an act of conservation finds itself inscribed within vestige itself. Here and there exist the first indications that the fetus, the stillborn, the dead nursling seem to have been invested with a status unto themselves. They're *withheld*, it would appear, from traditional burial rites and all that those rites suggest in terms of severance, removal, spiritual transmutation. However, it's not until fifteen hundred years later—with the advent of iron and the immense cultural transformations that immediately ensue— that this practice becomes current, not to say exclusive. From that moment forth, perinatal remains virtually disappear from both tumuli and necropolises. Domestic inhumation in small earthen pits without any accompanying grave goods becomes, for six consecutive centuries, standard practice. Indeed, evidence of this practice becomes apparent throughout the entire western Mediterranean, from the Iberian Peninsula to the Italic, from Valencia to Latium.

What exactly happened to render this form of infant burial so common, turning it—at this given, historical moment (about 700 B.C.)—into a recurrent, perfectly codified practice of its own? In way of response, we might consider some of the cultural transformations that were occurring at this time and the consequences they must have had on the psychic life of the communities involved. For iron not only brought with it the obvious advantages of a new technology (harder, sharper, more resistant tools derived from an abundant, readily available ore), but—ineluctably—a mentality of its own. This is apparent, today, in the archeological evidence yielded by any number of excavated sites throughout the western Mediterranean. What, in fact, has this evidence revealed? In the words of Michel Py, we become witnesses to a "spectacular acceleration" in the structural life of these Iron Age communities at this particular time.[4] Everything, it seems, undergoes consummate change. Out of small, agropastoral, self-sustaining societies, we witness the emergence of larger and larger "microstates," with highly fortified villages—*oppida*—on the spurs, ridges, and rock outcrops in the hinterland above. Practicing for the first time an agrarian economy based on surplus, these societies would come to store that surplus in granaries (underground silos or vast, terra-cotta *dolia*) within the fortified *oppida* themselves. That surplus would be exchanged against other goods in the first verifiable market economy in Mediterranean Gaul.

Who were they, we might ask ourselves? Did these emergent, mercantile societies belong to the same stock as those agropastoral communities that had subsisted throughout the Bronze Age in such small, autarkic structures? Nothing's less likely. Indeed, everything suggests the influx of an alien culture, most certainly from the northeast—most probably Celts or their immediate predecessors. We have, quite suddenly, an instance of cultural, social, ethnic "overlay": the superimposition of one order upon another. Concurrently, traces of social hierarchization become more and more apparent. Dwellings, for the first time, begin to vary in size, as do the tombs themselves, suggesting an emergent class structure. Progressively, the early Iron Age becomes a period in which "a complexification of interrelations will accompany a probable heterogenization of the social fabric."[5] Highest in this emergent structure would come the "agro-warrior," as Py has called him: a petty chieftain who lived both by the plowshare and the sword. Evidence, now, of a "warrior culture" becomes increasingly manifest everywhere, especially in the necropolises where the warrior himself is buried—cremated—side by side with his sword.

Archeology can often tell us much more about the mentalities of vanished cultures from the manner in which those cultures buried their dead than from the remnants of their day-to-day lives. Here, for instance, in this transitional moment between the Bronze and Iron Ages, we learn that incineration slowly, progressively, and finally exclusively replaces inhumation. As it does, the once plentiful "objects of accompaniment" tend to disappear in favor of a few rare, increasingly symbolic offerings such as a bowl or a goblet, suggesting the growing importance of libatory rites. "The ossuary itself disappears altogether in the fifth century B.C.," Py tells us, as "the incinerated remains—often nothing more than a symbolic handful of ashes—get scattered over an open ditch."[6]

Might I suggest, in light of all this, that families and particularly mothers belonging to those earlier autochthonic, agropastoral societies might well have refused to offer up the pathetic remains of their miscarried fetuses, stillborn babies, dead nurslings to so much alien, alienating ritual? Everything indicates a powerful atavistic reaction on their part, a resistance in letting these tiny corpses undergo—in the original sense of the word—"translation": transference, that is, from one place or condition to another; or—as in classic eschatology—from a "here" to a "hereafter." It's the *terms* of that translation, imposed by a warrior culture practicing universal incineration, that these earlier, subjected societies might well have rejected. Rejected, at least, for those who aroused the greatest emotion: the infant dead.

Furthermore, we may speculate that these very societies, still lingering in the agropastoral traditions of the late Bronze Age, might have deliberately refused, for their infant dead, *any* form of ritual burial whatsoever. The vestiges alone, as we've seen, reveal a total absence of ceremony. Nothing in these pit burials indicates the least attempt at "translation." The tiny body was laid—in fetal contraction—into the pit without any accompanying provision for its "afterlife." Even the earth with which it was covered—charged with broken pottery and culinary detritus—was not subject, it would seem, to the least act of selection, purification. Nor was the smallest hollow, the slightest cavity provided to store these infant deposits. Earth—thoroughly compacted—came to cover the defunct in a single, undifferentiated mass.

Isn't it possible that these sites are evidence of a counter-ritual, an anti-rite, a clear and categorical refusal on the part of these indigenous societies to admit to the separability of their ill-fated offspring? How could those who'd never lived or scarcely lived be subject to an afterlife as defined by an alien, invasive culture, imposing—along with incineration—an ever more remote, abstract vision of that very afterlife? No, to the contrary, these infant remains needed to be housed, coveted, planted like so many tubers in the pounded mud floors of the habitats themselves. Needed to be withheld in a tight, one-to-one symbiosis with substance itself, to be endowed—as such—with the status of "inseparables."

Yes, for the archeologist, the past—no matter how remote—has always laid at the tip of some glittering instrument, the nozzles of so many meticulously sweeping microvacuums. What makes the archeological discoveries in Languedoc so meaningful, however, aren't the vestiges themselves, but what they imply in terms of human comportment. For twenty-five hundred years after the fact, modern archeology has unearthed minute, irrefutable evidence of a most particular psychic disposition. For here, in the *garigues*, the hinterlands, of southern France, those who'd never (or scarcely) even existed were laid into these tiny earthen pits to await—across so much posthumous space—the only translation to which they could have possibly been subject: that of existence itself. For these planted little corpses, there could have been no "hereafter"—quite clearly—but "here"; no "afterlife" but "life" alone. Buried, they could have only awaited—within the bound world of the disconsolate—rebirth itself.

Terremare ☙

Each of us, I suspect, cherishes a particular landscape that outwardly reflects some all-too-invisible condition within. Its very topography gives color, contour, dimension to otherwise inaccessible areas of inner reality. Endows them with palpable configuration. Were I to select, say, a particular landscape of my own, I'd choose the broad, saline expanses of the Languedocian marshlands—most especially the northern rim of the archeologically rich Etang de l'Or. For there, in a wasteland of abandoned shacks and shooting blinds, its waters oily with eels, I found, as nowhere else, a mirror to a whole, evanescent world within.

I'd have preferred hills: preferred the far more temperate landscape of terraced orchards, overhanging vineyards. It's not a question, however, of preference, of personal taste, but one far deeper, that touches upon the quality of disclosure itself. If a particular landscape *speaks*, it's because that particular landscape has something to say.

We enter those flat, saline expanses—which lie between the open saltwater lake (*l'étang*) on one side and the first, firmly grounded apple orchards on the other—with caution. Rimmed in quicksand and subject to heavy seasonal flooding (*transgressions maritimes*), they do little to reassure the rare visitor. To the contrary, everything in these parts suggests the tenuous, the unstable. Suggests a nature that's left us little more than so much shifting ground underfoot. In this inhospitable mélange of earth and water, one has trouble enough fraying a passage, let alone imagining some erstwhile form of human habitation. An unexpected volley of slow, lackadaisical egrets only adds to that general impression. They flutter a few meters upwind, then settle once again behind a hedge of flowering pink tamarisks. It's their territory, not ours. We only enter these marshlands, we realize, as intruders.

And yet, in the late 1960s, a series of protohistoric sites was discovered lying like the beads of a broken rosary clear across the breadth of these very wetlands. Called terremare from the Italian *terra marna* (a rich, dark earth caused by the decomposition of organic substance, associated originally with an early Indo-European culture that had settled in the Po Valley), these communities, located in apparent wasteland, were discovered one after another. Altogether, eighteen separate habitats have been identified so far. Each belongs to a period that runs from the late Bronze to the early Iron Ages (that is, from the eleventh through the sixth century B.C.). For nearly six hundred consecutive years, we learn, humankind once dwelt in the midst of these paludal expanses. But how, we might ask ourselves? And, for our own incursive purposes, where? Where exactly?

Topographically, these eighteen excavated sites, spread out over an area of fourteen kilometers, share two common characteristics. First, they're invariably located alongside a fresh watercourse (a brook, creek, or small river) and usually within a few hundred meters of its outlet: where the watercourse, that is, meets the saltwater *étang*. Thus situated, their inhabitants would have been provided with an unlimited source of fresh water as well as an immediate access to the fishing beds beyond. Furthermore, the watercourses and the *étang*, taken as an aquatic ensemble, would have furnished them with a natural network of communication, perfectly suited for flat-bottom boats. Boats such as these might well have resembled the *sandolos* one sees today plying across the Venetian Lagoon.

It's the second topographical characteristic shared by these eighteen sites, however, that distinguishes them most. For each of them lies at an altitude that varies between 50 and 150 centimeters above sea level: at a height, that is, that's scarcely detectable. In entering these marshlands, one needs to be armed not merely with wading boots, precise documentation, and geodetic survey maps but also, if possible, with a natural flair for the geomantic sensing of particulars. For it's far too easy in these parts to miss the archeologically charged mound or *taparas* altogether. Far too easy, indeed, to miss the eloquence of all that vestigial deposit in the midst of so much steady, undermining sludge just beneath.

Here I am, then, moving in small, deliberate steps over a patch of scarcely consolidated marshland. Here, in a world of low-lying halophytes, of saltbush and sea lavender, I'm attempting to detect the slightest inclination in a resolutely flat expanse, trusting less to eyesight than the least pressure of the ground against instep, ankle, calf. And, sure enough, after several hundred meters, I begin sensing those first, nearly imperceptible signals—twinges, really—rising from the instep upward. They're not illusory. For there, at that very moment, among the occasional bottle caps and empty cartridge shells, among the shattered glass left by generations of itinerant duck hunters, I start spotting them: the unmistakable traces of early, protohistoric cultures. I'm no more than thirty centimeters, now, over the waterline, and yet they're already apparent: the somber, rough-cast fragments of hand-coiled Iron Age ceramic ware. As that minuscule gradient continues, my "finds" become more and more frequent. More and more abundant. I've clearly entered, now, the very heart of that abandoned habitat.

I'm fully aware, though, that anything I might discover on the surface of the ground has long since suffered displacement (*remaniement*): nothing's found where it "should be." Along with a total absence of human occupation for the past two-and-a-half millennia, tidal incursion has shifted the location of any given artifact so entirely that anything one might find lying on or close to the surface can only be considered, in contextual terms, as eccentric. It's only below, in the excavated depths of these terremare, that we can begin to appreciate the archeological wealth that we're only skimming here on the surface. It's in reaching backward, reading downward, searching through the appropriate documentation that we can begin to evaluate the magnitude of such a precarious culture.[1] Can begin to interpret the true sense of these potsherds, smelling of brine and burnt anise and lying at no distance whatsoever from total obliteration.

Often archeology functions in an opposite way from memory. Here, for instance, in the marshlands of these outlying terremare, the further down we explore, the more intact (or, at least, the more intrinsic) the vestige becomes. At a given depth, the trace—fortuitous at the surface—grows more and more manifest, conclusive. Thus, in working downward through so many layers of subsoil (the sediment itself turning from ocher to black as the underlying water

*Fragments of Iron Age pottery rise to the earth's
surface after high-water tides have subsided.
Photo by the author.*

table is approached) archeologists in the 1970s unearthed indisputable evidence
of nearly six hundred years of continuous occupation. This evidence, curiously
enough, lay in extraordinarily thin, laminal layers. If a particular archeological stratum could be said to vary, here, between ten and fifteen centimeters, the
stratum itself, in turn, could be subdivided into a plethora of mini-strata. What,
in fact, did these nearly negligible, tissuelike aggregations indicate?

It would seem that this occupation was rhythmic, seasonal. These lagoonal
sites were only inhabited, apparently, during the dry summer months. In autumn, high tides, heavy rains, and a subsequent rise in the underlying water

table would not only inundate the scanty settlements themselves but also lay a thin sedimentary film across the vestiges that's still detectable today. The vestiges are mostly ceramic. The earliest, dating from the middle Bronze Age (about 1500 B.C.), earlier, therefore, than the settlements themselves, are remarkably thick, predominantly black, and speckled white with crushed calcite crystals. The calcite, extracted no doubt from the limestone plateaus that lie at a considerable distance inland, served as a tempering agent. Occasionally, however, the calcite would be replaced by crushed seashell. This indicates that the *terramaricoles* might well have fired clay in situ, employing whatever materials happened to be close at hand: that is, the shells themselves.

Along with an abundant quantity of potsherds, archeologists have unearthed innumerable fragments of daubed wall (*torchis*), enough to suggest how these marsh dwellers once constructed their provisional, wood-framed shelters. Occasionally the clay fragments still bear the imprint of a long since vanished shaft of cane: a silent witness to one of their crosshatched supports. Occasionally, too, a number of hefty beach cobbles have been unearthed from the lowest stratigraphic levels. The cobbles could only have served, no matter how ineffectively, as ballast against the shifting ground on which these communities constructed (or reconstructed, each summer) their ephemeral dwellings.

Nothing, though, illustrates the precariousness of those dwellings quite so much as their hearths. Lying flush against the floor, be it of beaten earth or daubed clay, the hearths once yielded up minuscule bits of baked, rubified matter. Splinters really, they're all that remain of those provisional kitchens, of the smoke that rose out of their chimneys in thin billowing columns. The splinters themselves, along with innumerable bits of burnt charcoal too light to withstand the repeated incursions of winter tides, have all been displaced by floatage. They're invariably found, today, far from their original points of emanation.

The splinters, the charcoal, the near-microscopic, detrital remainders of mullet, sea bass, crayfish: could anything testify more poignantly to the extreme fragility of human habitat in general? Discovered at a depth very close to that of sea level, these vestiges of a long-since extinguished culture might serve to remind us, today, of the immensely delicate balance that must be met by any society in its relation to all the forces, natural or not, by which it's surrounded.

༄

Each archeological layer, as we've learned, is immediately followed by a layer of alluvium. These alternate deposits, composed of sand, salt crystals, minuscule gravel, and seashell, have been described by the specialists as "maritime contributions." Altogether, the successive layers, both archeological and alluvial, read somewhat like a book in which every other page contains some form of human inscription. Wedged between two inarticulate pages, the inscriptions have proven immensely informative.

If only the vaguest traces of ceramic dating from the middle Bronze Age have been detected, it's toward 1100 B.C. that signs of a continuous habitation on a seasonal basis become increasingly evident. From this period, one can date the earliest vestiges of daubed wall construction on crosshatched cane framework. One may assume that during this period, as well, the first significant attempts were made on the part of these *terramaricoles* to reclaim marshland, draining whatever areas they could for the sake of creating land fit for both pasture (they most certainly came with their flocks) and a brief season's subsistence agriculture.

By 900 B.C., the pages of this interpaginated book would begin speaking of an entirely new culture. Indo-European and most probably Celt or proto-Celt, this culture—the Urnfield—was named after the manner in which these people buried the ashes of their incinerated dead. Emerging out of eastern Europe, they'd have moved in a slow, assimilative migration westward, creating those very first terremare settlements in the marshlands of the Po. Were they a people drawn by nature—by genetic impulse—toward the terraqueous? It's quite possible, given their Danubian origins. Here, in any case, they left traces of their distinctive cinerary urns: between two layers of sludge, their cultural imprint is unmistakable. Continuing westward, they'd establish themselves eventually along the Catalonian coastline, creating the basic substratum of an emergent Celto-Iberian civilization.

As mentioned, each of these sites was located alongside a brook or little river for both an unlimited supply of fresh water and an immediate access onto the lagoon just beyond, teeming with fish and mussel. Toward the middle of the seventh century B.C., however, yet another advantage would be added, for at this time the first squat Etruscan coasting vessels appeared. Trafficking in wine and fine ceramic and bronze ware, they'd constitute the earliest vectors of classic Mediterranean civilization to reach southern Gaul. This initial contact would prove all-determinate to the life of the terremare. The sheer abundance of Etruscan wine amphoras and sophisticated *bucchero nero* ceramics speaks for itself. Today, examining the earthenware of those consecutive centuries, we become witnesses to a sudden cultural influx on a massive scale.

This influx, as interpreted by an increasingly accurate reading of the thin laminal microstrates, accelerates considerably through the seventh and sixth centuries B.C. Now, not only shattered bits of Etruscan earthenware can be identified, but fragments of Ionian, Rhodian and, soon after, Corinthian pottery as well. Indeed, here on the terremare, one can trace the gradual "Hellenization of Gaul," as the critical point of emanation of that culture moves

steadily westward out of Asia Minor and the Greek islands to the Greek main-
land, then, ultimately, to its all-dominant colony Massalia, no more than eighty
kilometers away.

Book, indeed. We've leafed through so many vestige-packed pages, the
pages interlaid with saline crystals, with the slime of tenacious deposit. It's as
if we had lying before us (whether in the sites themselves or in the documentation) the material evidence of some immensely rich allegorical property. For
here, memory and obliteration, the mnemonic and the lethean, seem interlocked
in a struggle that each has uninterruptedly waged with the other.

Vestiges begin thinning from about 525 B.C., and vanish altogether by the
end of that century. Certainly one can still find traces, here and there, of some
minor, sporadic, Gallo-Roman settlement several centuries later, but the intense annual occupation of these lagoonal settlements ended forever in the sixth
century B.C. Along with it disappeared the protohistoric culture of these lim-
inal communities. What, in fact, happened? Prehistorians are quite divided on
the subject, but one may assume that these settlements were definitively abandoned for reasons that were both natural and historic. Analyses of stratigraphic
deposits, drawn from that final period, have indicated a definite rise in the water table and, concurrently, a marked invasion of homometric beach cobbles
and conchiferous waste. A prolonged period of dampness seems to have ensued, rendering the marshlands uninhabitable.

At the same time, the neighboring Greek colony of Massalia, first settled
in 600 B.C., would have flourished into a major emporium. Establishing trade
routes of its own that connected this new-found colony to key marketplaces
throughout southern Gaul, Massalia would isolate the terremare altogether and
their minor, if indispensable, exchanges with the rest of the Mediterranean.
The terremare were removed, now, from the major axes of development and

were thus thoroughly marginalized. A spectacular rise in trade and an ensuing climate of competition, conflict, and insecurity that any sudden influx of capital creates would oblige those indigenous populations to settle in perched, heavily fortified *oppida* upland. Dwelling, now, behind the ramparts of hastily built defensive structures, these societies would protect not only themselves, but an ever-increasing quantity of goods, stocked in underground silos or vast terra-cotta *dolia*. There, those goods would await eventual exchange in a burgeoning, market-oriented economy.

Within no time the terremare would have suffered obsolescence, abandonment. Their inhabitants, who'd once enjoyed a basically self-sufficient existence, feeding on mullet, turtle, and squid each summer, as well as boar, deer, and oxen, would have fallen victim to an economy increasingly based on a network of interdependent exchanges between one microstate and another. The arrival of those first squat Etruscan coasting vessels would have ultimately proved fatal. For it marked the beginning of the end of these relatively autonomous, bucolic communities, living along the water's edge and subsisting, each summer, on nothing more nor less than what nature itself provided.

Each of us, I suspect, has a landscape of our own. And if I've chosen that of the terremare as the tangible manifestation of some all-too-invisible territory within, it's due, no doubt, to the very evanescence of the sites themselves. Lying only centimeters above so much continual tidal wash and subject each winter to total submersion, they reflect like nowhere else the very conditions of our own all too fragile, all too provisional existence: our so-called being here.

Having read all the documentation available, exploring therein the "memory" contained in the protohistoric subsoils, I returned, this spring, to the terremare themselves. Between reeds and rushes, in that half-world where the mounds scarcely protrude over the glistening surface of the waters, I once again began finding the ceramic vestiges of that vanished people. Drawn upwards by capillary action, the potsherds lay like eloquent reminders of—mementos to—that extreme precariousness. That existential edge. Each of them bore witness to a temporary convergence of seemingly haphazard determinants upon which any civilization (*ours* as much as *theirs*) attempts to ground itself.

Abandoned by even the archeologists, the sites are rarely visited these days. Wading across the *graus*, those innumerable little irrigation ditches that crosshatch the entire region, I had the distinct impression that the marshlands had been abandoned by everything but their birds. I spotted curlews, avocets, oyster-catchers, not to mention that flock of egrets that had settled on the opposite side of a stand of flowering tarmarisk. By far the most spectacular, however, were whole colonies of slender, spindle-legged flamingoes. Ruffled rose by a light, oncoming mistral, they scarcely moved as I approached. Studious, thoroughly intent on the abundant shell life at the tip of their tapering beaks, nothing seemed to disturb them. As I drew even closer, I came to realize that they'd become the true custodians of these abandoned sites. It was *their* territory, now, not ours.

Hadn't they, after all, been the first inhabitants of these terremare? Here they were, now, the very last. I went about making my collections, nonetheless, gathering irrefutable evidence of a culture that had once inhabited a thin spit of land, halfway between the high wind-washed sky overhead and the sky's reflection dissolving across the very waters before me.

On the Longevity of Toponyms ⤡

Nothing's older, in many places, than the toponyms themselves. Not even the archaic sites they still, occasionally, designate: the ruins, the earthworks, the beheaded remainders, say, of some *oppidum* lying perched on its long since abandoned outcrop. *Nomen*, quite frequently, antedates *habitatio*, for a partic- ular place was often named—attributed—prior to being settled. Thus the to- ponym constitutes an artifact of its own, a "document," as the scholars would put it. Nothing, in turn, receives more focused attention, not even the potsherds, the stray coin, the scrupulously analyzed cross sections of the carpolithes (the fossilized fruit of the site's earliest inhabitants). As the founding vocable, the toponym is treated with all the care of an immensely delicate, perfectly irre- placeable object.

An object? Can a word, a locution, a breath-shred be endowed with all the properties—the material attributes—of an object? Containing everything that might be found, eventually, within its sonorous outlines, can it be considered, indeed, as the object of objects, the "thing" preeminent?

Like the archeologist, the toponymist goes under. Searches, in the present-day place name, for some archaic particle, some linguistic vestige that has somehow managed to survive its lost origins. In a Mediterranean culture such as that of Provence, these origins are likely to be deeply secreted. Under successive layers of French, Provençal, and Latin (both medieval and classic), not to mention the "alluvial contributions" of Celtic and, to a lesser extent, Greek and Phoenician, one reaches, occasionally, a deposit—a material deposit—of an otherwise extinct language: Ligurian. Spoken by a people of that name, indigenous to the present-day provinces of Liguria in northwestern Italy and Provence in southeastern France, their linguistic group has been identified as pre–Indo-European. Their language forms a "substratum," as the toponymists would put it. Like an archeological foundation or baseline, it's upon this Ligurian substratum that successive cultures—in successive, toponymical layers—have left their deposits. Even if we know next to nothing about the Ligurian culture itself, we can fairly well assume that certain sounds, embedded in certain place names, belong to these vanished people. It's nearly all, in fact, that has survived them.

When we refer to particular places, for example, we might find ourselves emitting—as breath particles—the radicals *ar-, kar-, tar-,* and so on. Little do we realize that we are employing the relics of that extinct idiom, perpetuating, in a sense, a lost culture. For out of those very radicals come the toponyms themselves: from *ar-* come Arles and Orange; from *kar-,* Carry, Cassis, and by extension, Carcassonne; from *tar-,* Tarascon, and so forth. What, in fact, do they signify, these linguistic fragments? As in all archaic languages, they indicate some topological feature: more often than not, one associated with rock or water. They might specify, for example, some mountain, ledge, or distinct counterfort, or—to the contrary—some stream, marshland, estuary. For these early toponyms served to distinguish the landscapes these protohistoric people inhabited, helped separate, in succinct locatives, high ground from low, their own pastureland from that of their neighbors, where they hunted from where they fished. In each instance the place name indicated some geophysical characteristic, and, by implication, the kind of economy practiced therein. The toponym "staked out" a particular area, circumscribed—with a sharp, evocative monosyllable—the material realities of the place itself. Sound, here, proclaimed substance; the toponym, its very *topos*.

How can we help but marvel at the work, say, of Vittorio Bertoldi,[1] tracing the pre–Indo-European radical *ganda-* to its origins, signifying "a rocky terrain as caused by a mountain landslide," or Pierre Fouché's study[2] of *kal* in all its multiple ramifications, indicating—in turn—a rock, a rock shelter, a dwelling, a fortress, and, finally, an entire village. In reading the great toponymists, don't we find our own mouth rounding, say, to the beautiful morpheme *eoo*, meaning—as well it might—a lake, a body of water? The morpheme still survives today in certain areas of the Pyrenees. In the language of the specialists, it's known as a "fossilized resonance."

We're not always so fortunate, however. Place names, as Charles Rostaing points out, have suffered all the vicissitudes of words in general.[3] Subject to wave after wave of acculturation, the original toponyms have undergone endless modifications if not—as in many cases—total effacement. As the "object of objects," they were shaped, altered, refashioned to fit the language—and the proclivities—of whatever culture happened to be dominant at any particular time. Ligurian, for instance, as an indigenous language, came to be assimilated with Celtic when the Celts infiltrated southeastern France in the sixth century B.C. The amalgamation, Celto-Ligurian, fell in turn under the influence of Greek. Along with the potter's wheel, the vine, and the olive tree, the Greeks brought with them the written alphabet. They affected the Celto-

Ligurians more by example than rule: traces of their immensely sophisticated culture would permeate the interior from the emporia they established along the coastline. One after another, place names along their trade routes underwent Hellenization. This would be followed, in the second century B.C., by the arrival of the Romans, by the Roman *mainmise* over Mediterranean Gaul. No alien culture would have such a determining influence. Needless to say, the toponym—that most susceptible of vocables—would undergo immense changes in what the Roman colonizers now called Provincia Romana. Truncating here, agglutinating there, Latinizing everywhere, the Romans would shape the name of the place as indelibly as they'd shape the place itself.

The toponym, however, still hadn't found its definitive form. Hadn't yet—in the language of the toponymists—"crystallized." One needs to follow the life of these sonorous objects through the fall of the Roman Empire and the abrupt arrival, at the same time, of barbaric invaders. Revelatory in its own right, a period of pure stasis ensues, a time of total cultural sterility. It would be followed (but quietly, slowly, almost subliminally) by a second Latinization, that of Christendom itself. Almost exclusively the "property" of ecclesiastics and, most especially, that of its scribes, this second Latinization would filter gradually into the living idiom. As it did, it would serve to evangelize one place name after another. Even now, though, these fresh nominals would be subject to endless alterations. Having undergone, all too often, the poetic fantasies of those very scribes mentioned above, they'd find themselves vernacularized as they entered into the regional dialects. For instance, a place name such as Sanctus Amantius would become, in Provençal, Sanch Amans. In popular usage (spoken rather than written), the *San* would find itself isolated and the truncated consonant, *ch*, undergo fusion with the succeeding *amans*, to form San Chamans. The commune is now called Saint-

Chamas in honor of Saint Amantius who, most probably, wouldn't recognize his own name today.

A toponym, at least in Mediterranean Europe, celebrates a series of elisions, adaptations, and, quite often, dissimulations rooted in over three thousand years of human history. Organic in its own right, its development is inseparable from all the forces that have contributed to its formation. All the more amazing, then, that a place name might still include—like a pearl on a string of dull, luster-less syllables—some archaic particle. Some irreducible relic. Surviving a culture that no longer exists, that particle calls to mind the rocks, riverbeds, defensive ledges upon which civilizations were first founded. It calls to mind—in a closing moment—lost origins.

II

Today, anyone arriving in Provence by air will land, most likely, at the airport of Marseille-Marignane. If a mistral happens to be blowing on that particular day, there's a good chance that the arriving passenger will get a whiff of the petrol refineries, located six kilometers to the northwest. It serves as a reminder. Even in the midst of a Provençal spring, with orchards of flowering fruit trees visible only minutes from the airport itself, that dark, acrid odor, blown through the bright air, reminds us of our own specific moment in history. No, we haven't escaped: not even here.

The refineries themselves surround—virtually suffocate—the little provincial town of Berre. Lying at the edge of a placid saltwater lake of the same name, the town was once destined for something far happier. It had been abundantly endowed with a natural resource: that of salt. Indeed, Berre meets all the conditions necessary for the exploitation of that indispensable mineral:

bright sun, a dry violent wind, and shallow marshes that contained, at one time, a higher rate of salinity than the Mediterranean: thirty-five grams of salt per liter of water. Along with an abundant quantity of fish, shellfish, and crustacea, salt must have attracted Berre's first protohistoric settlers. A precious element in itself, it became, along with tin, the most highly prized commodity in a barter-based economy. Soon after Caesar's conquest of Gaul, Berre, settled by Roman legionnaires, would evolve along the edge of one of the *viae salariae*, the imperial "salt routes" that Rome had established across the western Mediterranean.

Berre's history, in many ways, resembles that of other towns along the French littoral. Pillaged by the Visigoths at the end of the fifth century, it would suffer eclipse through the Dark Ages and gradually resuscitate with the new millennium. As a duchy from the Middle Ages to the Revolution and the *chef-lieu* of its canton ever since, Berre has prospered from its own natural endowments and especially that of its salt deposits. Indeed, one tends to forget at the end of this millennium how autonomously most communities once subsisted, how self-sufficing their economies. In short, how *rooted* they once were to their own natural, immediately available, abundantly regenerative, resources. Berre was no exception.

Since 1929, however, this history has tended to reverse itself. With the installation of the first petrol refineries in its suburbs and the inexorable rise of an adjacent petro-chemical complex, the air of this lovely, lake-facing community has literally darkened. Worse, that same air has grown charged with the microorganic particles of an uninterrupted pollution. Those who control the valves and maintain the machinery in this massive complex have become its very first victims. Ecologically, culturally, and, inevitably, economically, the site— invaded by immense capital investment from without—has suffered severe degradation. Today, Berre, as a community, can only watch itself go under, and in the process lose all possible claim to its own innate character. Quite suddenly, Berre might be anywhere in the blighted landscapes of the postindustrial.

Every bit as injurious as the pollution of its atmosphere has been that of its waters. A power plant belonging to the Electricité de France was constructed along the edge of the Etang de Berre only twelve kilometers to the west. Shedding millions of square meters of fresh water into the saltwater lake, it has virtually destroyed most of the lake's native flora and fauna and driven its rate of salinity down to practically nothing. Only a few years ago, this same body was rife with flamingoes, oyster catchers, avocets. They'd nest among the bulrushes and feed on a plethora of bivalves, gastropods, and tiny scampering crustaceans. Today this natural life no longer exists. The Etang de Berre lies like a vast, glistening tomb, honoring, if anything, its own past. Soon, we're told, these fresh waters, carrying in their cataract an inordinate amount of silt, will bring the lake—ironically enough—to total desiccation. Soon they'll gag the lake altogether with effluent.

Along with the death of any ecological entity comes that of the economy it once generated. In the case of the Etang de Berre, this economy—based essentially on the exploitation of its salt pans and its abundant marine fauna—had thrived since the early Iron Age. Had existed in a state of biotic equilibrium for nearly three thousand years. This balance was swept aside in a matter of moments by the signing of a contract and the consequent implantation of numerous industries. These industries, of course, having exhausted whatever advantages they originally found in the immediate area, or having simply depleted its ecology, can always move elsewhere. Berre, to the contrary, cannot. Like many other communities throughout the world, Berre will have to live in the midst of its own spoliation.

Berre, we might hear ourselves uttering. As inveterate dilettantes in the science of toponymy, we find ourselves, often enough, searching for roots—the archaic radicals of given place names—hoping to discover, at the heart of an appellation, some vague trace of its origins. For "every place name," Rostaing tells us, "has its own signification, even if that signification has long been lost to its own inhabitants."[4]

Berre, in French, evolved out of *Berro*, in Provençal. If Auguste Vincent attributes its origin to *Berra* in low Latin, meaning "plain" or "valley,"[5] Frédéric Mistral, flirting momentarily with the Semitic radical *beer-*, settles finally for a more indigenous interpretation: what signifies, in pre-Celtic, "a place situated alongside water."[6] D. Fletcher Valls goes even deeper. By drawing on the pre-Indo-European substrate, he associates the radical *ber-* with *ibère*, and, by extension, *Iberia:* the land, that is, of the Iberi.[7] These people, it should be noted, were not only contemporary with the Ligurians, but belonged, culturally speaking, to the same linguistic group: both constituted integral parts of what has come to be called a "Mediterranean unity." It's quite possible, Valls speculates, that *ber-* originally evolved into (or out of) *berro*, meaning nothing more nor less, in present-day Spanish, than watercress. A wild variety of that very plant is still to be found—curiously enough—in Berre's last surviving marshland. It goes, needless to say, unpicked.

Berro, Berra, Berre: the vocable gets blown out of the darkness of its own disputed origins. Surviving its very history—the depredations to the very place it designates—it contains, in that brief monosyllable, the breath of its own inception. The sign-initiate. Even today, spoken more often than not by immigrant workers—Algerians, for the most part, imported as cheap labor in the fifties and suffering today from massive unemployment—the word, the toponym itself, breaks through an otherwise uninterrupted stream of Arabic. Or, in the groping French of a Dutch technician, flown in by Shell Petroleum to solve some obscure malfunction at the refineries, *Berre* resounds through so much hesitation, *maladresse*, as his one unmistakable utterance.

Aren't we always, in a sense, resuscitating the oldest sounds—be they toponyms or not—for our own most immediate purposes? Utilizing, over and over, archaic particles for the sake of some pressing circumstance? Some impending issue? As to the sounds themselves, don't they invariably contain—even at this incalculable distance—the grain, the germ, the invisible seedpod of those incipient cultures they once initiated? We enter our own darkness, today, uttering them. Enter the opacity of our times breathing into sheer air the transparent relics of those lost dawns. Carry them—tinkling like amulets—into whatever future the future still holds.

The Cult of Skulls 🖋

FROM SEVERANCE TO SCULPTURE

"They embalm the heads of their enemies in juniper oil then flaunt them before the eyes of their guests. They refuse, in way of exchange, even the heads'
very weight in gold."[1] So wrote the Greek geographer, Strabo, in describing
Celto-Ligurian tribesmen who inhabited strongholds in the hills of Provence
from the fifth to second centuries B.C. Who were they and in what kinds of
barbarous rites did they indulge? Were they, indeed, an "atrocious people," as
one contemporary eyewitness described them?[2] Were they a "society of head-
hunters," as a modern historian has put it?[3]

Celto-Ligurian: the amalgam alone raises questions. For Celts and Ligurians sprang from two totally disparate cultures. The Celts, an Indo-European
people who emanated from central Europe and infiltrated southern France
some time in the sixth century B.C., brought with them a highly evolved, hierarchical social structure and a whole set of advanced skills ranging from metal
craft to charioteering. The Ligurians, on the other hand, were autochthonous.

Inhabiting perched sites above the Mediterranean coastline since the Neolithic, they were overwhelmed, it would seem, by the far more sophisticated,
dynamic culture propagated by the Celts. Together, as a gradually assimilated
people, they came to observe the same rites, worship the same divinities.
Whether the particular kind of skull veneration they both commonly practiced
originated with the Celts or Ligurians remains to be determined. In any case,
the cult quickly took on considerable magico-religious significance. In sites
such as Roquepertuse, Entremont, and La Cloche, considerable numbers of
skulls have been discovered totally removed from any funerary context whatsoever, but in close topological association with the sanctuaries themselves.
Clearly, the skulls were the object—the "sensate receptacles," as one archeologist put it[4]—of a particular form of worship.

As the severed heads, presumably, of enemy warriors, these "trophies" were
either embalmed in oil or coated in fresh clay. They were then left on exhibit
in egg-shaped alcoves carved especially for the purpose within the monolithic
columns and overriding lintels of the sanctuary proper. More than simply displayed, these skulls were enshrined. Today, lodged once again in the alveoli of
colonnades that have been patiently reassembled in the Musée de la Vieille
Charité, Marseilles, these decomposed heads possess a barbarous magnetism,
for they still manage to inspire that most archaic of all psychic reactions: ambivalence itself. Holding us between repulsion and respect, terror and defer-
ence, we're still, it would seem, affected by these gutted husks. Much like the
mask of the gorgon, the skulls belong neither to this world nor the next, but
to that wavering interface, that intermediary realm between being and non-
being, the living and the dead. Threshold figures, they command passage.

The earliest irrefutable example of a skull treated as both a separate entity
and a venerated object dates from the Mousterian (about 50,000 B.C.). The skull,

belonging to a Neanderthal, was discovered without any anatomical connection in the Grotto of Guattari at Mount Circe, Italy, in 1939. It had been deliberately, even delicately, laid into a circle of stones prepared for its reception. Examples such as this are extremely rare in the Paleolithic. Another would be the skull of a woman found at Le Mas-D'Azil and dating from the Magdalenian (about 12,000 B.C.), her empty eye sockets studded with carved bone to simulate a gaze. Whenever such examples arise, the skull itself should be considered a relic or reliquary, not a trophy. It should be attributed, that is, to ancestor worship rather than to a cult based on the deliberate acquisition of magical properties. This holds true throughout the Neolithic. For example, skulls discovered at Mureybet along the banks of the Euphrates were originally mounted on small clay pedestals along the walls of domestic sanctuaries. There, as the venerated heads of ancestors, they were left on display. Throughout the Fertile Crescent, from Byblos on the Phoenician coast to central Anatolia, heads such as these have been discovered modeled in lime (Halaf), impregnated in tar and enveloped in a braided hair net (Nahal Hemar), or richly inlaid with cowrie shells (Jericho). At a necropolis at Beidha, archeologists were surprised to discover a number of beheaded skeletons lying in the stone coffers they'd just unearthed. It would appear that the population, upon abandoning the site, had taken their most venerable possessions—the skulls—along with them.

It's not until we reach the Iron Age proper that the "Cult of Skulls" comes to be associated with headhunting. It should be noted, however, that despite the immense generic difference between the severed head of an enemy warrior and that of a beloved kin, both were invested with transcendent powers. As "sensate receptacles," both possessed hierophantic values far exceeding those of simple keepsakes. To the contrary, they were actively charged with the propitiatory: with the talismanic virtues of an interceding agent, be it in favor of an individual, a family or a clan (as with the skulls of ancestors), or an entire tribe (as with the skulls of enemies). In each of these cases, they afforded "protection, abundance and fertility," in Fernand Benoit's words, to those fortunate enough to possess them.[5]

Along with the expansion of the so-called Warrior Cultures in the Iron Age, the practice of headhunting spread commensurately. From the *oppidum* of Puig-Castellar in Spain to Stanwick in Yorkshire, England, skulls have been discovered that hung once from metal hooks at the entrance to settlements. They were charged, no doubt, with those same expiatory powers mentioned above. Within Celtic mythology alone, don't we have an entire "literature of decapitation," as one historian has put it?[6] One only need mention Cu Chulain's exploits in the *Tain* or the severed head of Brân in the *Mabinogion* which spoke out and assured its captors of the joys of unending prosperity.

The Celto-Ligurian *oppida* in Provence have yielded evidence, however, of yet a further level of development in the magico-religious treatment of the human head. At some point between the beginning of the third and the end of the second century B.C., we have, in Brigitte Lescure's words, "that crucial moment of passage from an expression based upon actual matter—the bones themselves—to one of plastic evocation: that is to say, sculpture."[7] We're moving, in that very moment, from fact to artifact and, in so doing, from substance to symbol: from the magical investment of matter to its semiotic representation. Certainly it's a moment through which all civilizations, if permitted, will transit. It's one in which they come to sublimate an earlier practice, based on a belief in the innate power of material objects, for that of their effigiation: sculpture, in this instance, replacing skulls. The severed head is rendered now in limestone, the hand of its captor (in several instances) running through the locks of its hair. In these Celto-Ligurian *oppida,* evidence of that transition,

Sculpted head of a beheaded Iron Age warrior.
The sculpture was cleaved by Roman invaders.
Photo courtesy Centre Camille Jullian, CNRS,
Université de Provence, Aix-en-Provence.

that moment in time, has come to light within little more than a few square meters of excavated space. That all-decisive event in the evolution of any culture has been circumscribed in places such as these a full twenty-three hundred years after the fact. Within a specific patch of meticulously inspected earth, the moment itself—one might say—has been isolated.

It should be noted, however, that the sculptures didn't entirely replace the severed heads: the cultic observation of both one and the other continued to coexist until the end of the Celto-Ligurian world itself. As irrefutable proof that severed heads continued to be taken, both skulls and sculptures have been unearthed at sites such as Entremont from the exact same stratigraphic levels. Other cults, other cultures have offered up similar examples of such parallel practices, venerating, simultaneously, organic substance and its graphic substitutes. Christianity, in its adoration of both the bones of its blessed, encased in reliquaries, and their images, glowing radiant from icons, embraces (as much as any religion) such parallel practices. The former, of course, antecedes the latter. As both a psychic and cultic phenomenon, the veneration of bones belongs to a far more archaic mode of worship. As deeply rooted as it is, could it ever, in fact, be fully suppressed, replaced, sublimated into a panoply of figurative equivalents?

Here, history itself will come to answer our questions, for in 123 B.C., a culture, infinitely more advanced and more sophisticated than that of the Celto-Ligurians—not only in terms of socioeconomic structure and technological achievement but also in regard to the elaboration of those "figurative equivalents"—destroyed these fortified hill villages, one after another. At the Musée Granet in Aix-en-Provence, there is more than adequate evidence of such devastation. It appears that the Roman army, in attacking *oppida* such as Roquepertuse, Entremont, and La Cloche, went directly after the sculptures themselves. Lobbing off noses and cheeks, sectioning entire necks, planting their axes squarely down the center of so many limestone skulls, they beheaded, disfigured, massacred the lifeless representations of a society's singular devotion. They not only laid low the population itself but the objects of its veneration, what the Celto-Ligurians had only recently managed to translate into sign, effigy, sculpture. In short, the works of an emergent society found themselves barbarized by a culture considered immeasurably more advanced. The sign, here, was taken for substance; the figuration, for figure.

One can only wonder, in the face of all this evidence, whether civilization represents anything more than its own tireless, often aborted efforts to "shore image": to bring its vision of the sacred, finally, into the shelter of some ineffaceable effigy. Here, for instance, within the context of a late Iron Age culture, we've followed the transition of one such vision as it went from the "sensate receptacle" of a severed head to its representation as sculpture. That transition has always depended on the sublimation of its subject. The final result, however—the sculpture itself—is far from being assured the kind of inviolability one might expect. Completed, it finds itself exposed to exactly the same conditions, vicissitudes, fates as the civilization it epitomizes. Sculpture can be shattered, frescoes obliterated, entire libraries burnt. What might only have been attained after an immense psychic effort on the part of a particular culture can be lost in no more time than it takes, say, to sack a small protohistoric citadel.

Here in these abandoned, wind-swept ruins that still ooze, occasionally, fractured bits of sculptured anatomy, we come to realize that we're not merely witnesses to the past. Whatever level of transfigurate expression we ourselves may have reached can be undone as swiftly as theirs was. A carved earlobe here, a nostril there—vestiges, we call them—come to remind us of this all too evident fact.

PART III

Under the Raised Trellises ᖇ

Negative Architecture 🖋

For anyone who lingers about ruins, there's invariably some structure—some solid, wind-pitted rampart, for instance—to admire, meditate upon. Here, though, in the Greco-Massalian quarries along the French littoral, no particular feature draws our attention if not the squares and rectangles of extracted volume, if not the hewn outlines, in fact, of a distinct counterstructure. For we've entered, architectonically speaking, a world in negative. We've wandered into a space that we can only read—and in reading, interpret—by attending to the eloquence of its voids. At La Pointe de l'Arquet in the *commune* of La Couronne, we might find ourselves staring at a jagged set of right angles carved out of some low limestone ledge. Isn't the right angle the very signature, the trace *par excellence* of human passage? Here, however, the sign doesn't indicate some small, incremental step in a given construction. To the contrary, it signifies depletion. Designates the geometric outlines of excavated mass.

We stand there, gazing down. Stand at the edge of this narrow, wind-blown

Greek quarries at La Pointe de l'Arquet.
Photo by the author.

peninsula, gazing at the tide as it invades the lowest levels of the quarry itself. It covers, in a thin, limpid sheath, the broad checkerboard pattern created over two thousand years earlier out of all those extracted sections. If anything, the tide tends to magnify those sections, exaggerate the already immense emptiness of the abandoned worksite itself. It's not every day, we realize, that we're allowed to gaze into the contours of absence, into the specific proportions, dimensions, properties that absence, under a given set of conditions, has assumed. Is memory any different? Aren't we continually running over the imprint, the deeply scored outlines of vanished experience, attempting to read—in counterpoint—the plenitude of so many irrecuperable events, reading *here* what's eternally *there*? It's not altogether different with the quarries. They once supplied Marseilles (Ionian Massalia) with the materials for its ramparts, administrative buildings, theaters, and temples. Furnished it, out of all these successive limestone layers, with its long lost architectural splendors. In either case, we're left—as readers—confronting lacunae: interpreting, as we go, volume from depleted vestige.

The earliest surviving mention of the site comes from Strabo. In his invaluable (if often inaccurate) *Geographica*, he wrote: "A bit further than Massalia, at about one hundred stadia [eighteen kilometers] from the city and lying against a rocky promontory [certainly that of La Chaîne de l'Estaque] these quarries face directly onto the coastline, just before the coastline itself curves inward to form the Gulf Gaulois."[1] Why there? We, as would-be historians— interpreting history by all this hollow human imprint, by the fossilization of so much arduous human effort—learn that this particular limestone was ideally suited for construction. Relatively easy to extract, to carve into six coherent surfaces, the blocks were remarkable for their high compressive strength. Furthermore, they were exceedingly handsome. Encrusted with opalescent oyster shell, the stone itself—Tertiary, Miocene—gave off a pale, ocher-rose cast. We can only imagine, today, how the facades of a temple dedicated to the much venerated Artemis must have appeared. Can only imagine how its pediment, the color of dawn, must have glowed under a deep mistral blue. Imagine, we say, because we only have these cratered outlines, now, to serve as witness: only the jagged edges of all these successive limestone shelves.

The fact that the quarries themselves are located alongside the coastline isn't, of course, fortuitous. Scows could moor flush alongside them in waters three meters deep. Indeed, one can still see notches carved into the bedrock to receive the cables of those vessels as they came to berth. Called by the Romans *naves lapidariae*, they could take up to three-and-a-half tons of cargo in their deep holds. If this seems like an inordinate amount for such times, we might consider the wreckage of the *Marʒamemi III*, sunk off the eastern coast of Sicily, which held twenty tons of granite destined for the temples of Thebes. We are, after all, studying a moment in which cultures expressed themselves in monumental terms. We shouldn't be surprised by either the magnitude of their undertakings or the extent of geological spoliation they occasioned. If the Greek sense of scale was harmonious and based on human proportion, its sense of mass—at the same time—was colossal.

Standing here, on the tip of this narrow peninsula, we can stare clear across the open waters to Marseilles itself. It lies at a distance of twenty-five kilometers (rather than the eighteen specified by Strabo). It would have been a direct run for those *naves*, hugging—if need be—the littoral in times of heavy weather. In fact, as we stand here, gauging the distance between quarry and building site—La Pointe de l'Arquet and Marseilles—it's safe to speculate that virtually every stone block that went into the construction of the antique city was, at one moment or another, afloat, buoyed in the wooden hull of some stout, shuttling cargo. Each ponderous volume must have displaced its own weight in a draft of deep underlying seawater.

We're fortunate, today, to have documentation on those volumes: on their extraction, transportation, and ultimate deployment. Of the volumes themselves, however, scarcely anything remains, only an Ionic column here, a bit of truncated rampart there, vestiges discovered quite by accident in excavating the antique city—not for itself, but for the sake of preparing the ground for modern high-rise office buildings. Nevertheless, these materials have provided the specialist with enough data to conduct their examinations and arrive at certain conclusions. For instance, geomorphologists have managed to compare in sophisticated laboratory analyses thin laminated strips of limestone taken from the antique blocks themselves with others, drawn from various areas in the quarry. They've managed to match one with the other: a specimen, say, from a shattered, bulldozed section of a once elegant entablature with that of a certain stratigraphic level at L'Arquet. They've been found to coincide with astonishing accuracy.

Other analyses, based on measure alone (metrological), have proved to be equally conclusive. Here, it's the dimensions of the blocks themselves that have undergone scrutiny. These incumbent masses have been measured against— compared with—their hollow counterparts in the quarries. The results of these analyses at first puzzled the specialists. For they discovered that the dimensions of the former (the blocks) didn't exactly match those of the latter (the hollows): that the masses were invariably a centimeter or two less than the hacked-out rectangles they'd created within the quarries themselves. It soon became evident that the blocks had been carved twice: first, by the quarrymen, the *latamoi*, at the quarry proper; then, after transport, by the stone carvers, the *lapicides*, working at the base of some rampart or along the plinth of some elegant oratory. There, each block, arriving rough-cast from the quarries, would be rasped, redressed, shaped to fit, with astonishing accuracy, its assigned place. This double preparation would account, of course, for the minute loss in the block's final dimensions: what has been measured, by the specialists, down to the last, seemingly inconsequential millimeter.

There's something touching, indeed, in all the care, the meticulous attention given, nowadays, to all this vestige. There's something disturbing, however, as well. We're far richer, today, in voids than in entities: in the mineral outlines of absence than the assembled masses that the absence once articulated. How, in fact, should we read this empty text, these low, outlying shelves at the Mediterranean's edge that the tide, now, has totally invested? In negative? Like a negative held, say, against the light? If so, it's one from which we might readily glean (in default of any existent print) an incisive image. For we have, after all, the hacked, chiseled, quoined profile of an entire vanished city lying before us like a text of sorts, written in its own particular idiom. Written in what might be called an inverted grammar. We must read it, *learn* to read it, like memory itself. Follow it, this very moment, over its flooded rectangles— rife with tiny propellant cuttlefish—as if we'd just entered the empty chambers of some long suppressed recollection.

No, it's not in Marseilles, in the dusty showcases of its museums or the sparse architectural fragments to be found in its Jardin des Vestiges, but here, in interpreting these lacunae, that we'll come to approach such losses. Come to appreciate, perhaps, their very magnitude. Bit by bit, we might even come to read, in that inverted grammar, the otherwise lost text of the sea city itself. An idiom of its own, it deserves our utmost attention.

Undulant-Oblique ❧

A STUDY OF WAVE PATTERNS ON
IONICO-MASSALIAN POTTERY

If wine, as we're told, allowed Mediterranean civilization to penetrate the still-protohistoric world of Provence, the history of wine cannot be disassociated from the amphoras in which it was transported, nor the cups, kraters, skyphos from which it was drunk.[1] For here, "contained" and "container" form a single cultural entity. Imported into Provence in the seventh century B.C. by both Etruscans and Phoenicians, wine and, inseparably, the clay vessels in which it came constituted—as barter—the single most sought-after commodity. With the arrival of the Ionians a century later, this trade increased considerably. For the Ionians not only exchanged goods with the indigenous populations (trading essentially wine, pottery, and bronze ware for tin, iron, and salt) but established emporia of their own for stocking and distributing those goods. The first and by far the most significant of those emporia—those fortified trading posts—was Massalia: present-day Marseilles.

Called by Herodotus the "progenitors of history," the Ionians were Greeks who had settled in Asia Minor and assimilated the cultures of kindred societies flourishing in those very regions. This assimilation would prove to be highly generative. Founding, in a short period of time, their own schools of philosophy, art, and architecture, inventing coinage, and propagating the acquisitions of an entirely original culture throughout the Mediterranean, they quickly became the radiant center of all Hellenism. Nothing they touched, it seems, wasn't marked by a natural sense of measure, grace, innate proportion, by what might be called, indeed, an "auroral intelligence."

Nowhere would the expression of that intelligence be more widely diffused than in their pottery and especially in the motifs with which that pottery was decorated. One particular motif, the wave pattern (misleadingly labeled in English the "wood pattern") seems particularly relevant. For there, in oscillating ripples, the Ionians would give expression to the very energies at play in that generative period of their evolution. Whether the ceramics in question happened to have originated in Ionia itself or in its new emergent colony to the west, Massalia, matters little, for in both cases the motif underwent a virtually identical evolution. In tracing that evolution, we find ourselves following—quite inadvertently—the vibratory weave of an originating vision. Find ourselves drawn, on oscillation alone, over the threshold of that inaugural occasion.

"For the fuller's screw, the way, straight and crooked, is one and the same."[2] So wrote Heraclitus, an Ionian himself, describing the apparent contradiction of opposites in the inseparable flow of the singular: that of Being. No statement more accurately describes the energies inherent in that undulant pattern. Written at the very moment the Ionian decor had come to free itself from certain "orientalizing" characteristics (manifest in static, geometric motif), it expressed the *fluidity* of the new philosophy. It spoke of a universe in continuous motion, change, in which "all things are driven through all others" by a single governing principle.[3] The waves, indeed, illustrate that principle. Existing in a harmony of "opposing forces," they, like Heraclitus's lyre, vibrate to a series of tensions and releases.[4]

Studying this particular motif in regional museums or in those rare archeological papers devoted to the Hellenization of Gaul, one is struck by a curious phenomenon. In the sixth century B.C.—at the beginning of the Ionian colonization of Marseilles—the wave pattern tends to oscillate freely, to ripple in a loose set of seemingly erratic intervals. Labeled by the archeologists as oblique, uneven, or irregular, it's generally dismissed by those specialists as something primitive if not, quite simply, maladroit. But is it? We seem to be in the presence, rather, of a graphic rendering of that very flux Heraclitus himself first evoked. In the presence, that is, of an incipient—emergent—energy flow, interpreted here through an artisanal medium. What the potter's hand, incising the freshly thrown clay, had delineated.

Flux, flow: we're reminded of the Greek infinitive, *rhein*, which describes this very movement, and which Emile Benveniste qualified as the "essential predicate" in Ionian philosophy from the time of Heraclitus onward. In Benveniste's luminous essay, "La notion de 'rythme' dans son expression linguistique," we learn that *rhein*, as generatrix of *rhitmos* (from which we derive *rhythm*), signifies the manner by which objects in nature are deployed, positioned, momentarily situated. In combining *rhein* (to flow) and the suffix *-thmos* (suggesting the mode by which a particular action is actively perceived by the senses), we arrive at the signifier for an immensely rich, immensely variable quantity. *Rhitmos*, at this diacritical moment in Western thought, isn't to be

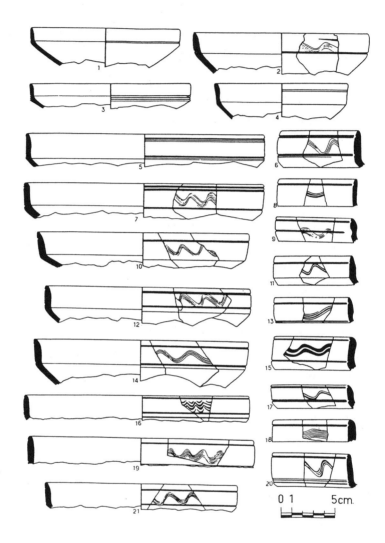

Examples of the wave pattern in Ionico-Massalian pottery. Courtesy Fonds Fernand Benoit, Palais du Roure, Avignon.

seen as some idea, some fixed, inalterable concept, but as the fluid architectonics of each given instance. "It designates form," in Benveniste's words, but "form as shaped by the mobile, the moving, the liquid; as something that possesses no organic consistency of its own. It is more like a pattern drawn across water, like a particular letter arbitrarily shaped, like a gown, a *peplos* casually arranged, or a sudden shift in an individual's mood or character." It constitutes form, certainly, but form as something "improvised, provisional, modifiable."[5]

How close this definition comes to describing the archaic wave pattern itself, so quickly dismissed by the specialists as something "irregular." To the contrary, the potter was giving free play not to his own whims and fancies but to the vibratory flow of yet unregulated energies. He was, we might call it, expressing himself in an ontological script, the calligraphy of *Logos* itself. The parallel lines he traced appear to rush, undulant, out of some immediate if invisible point of origin. They rise, plummet, exult—convulsively—about the flanks of some terra-cotta vase like a freshly released creature. If anything, they seem *alive*.

Here we're very close to a vision of existence that, after being rapidly suppressed, would have to wait two and a half millennia to see itself reasserted. How familiar it sounds to readers of Nietzsche's *Philosophy in the Tragic Age of the Greeks* or—more immediately—Heidegger's *Being and Time*. We might be reminded, too, in the realm of modern aesthetics, of Klee's definition of art as *Gestaltung*: as form in the perpetual process, or act, of formation. Or Olson's interpretation of the poem as a "high-energy construct" in which "form is never more than an extension of content."[6] These, indeed, are archaic canons. Together, they share a common vision. Within that vision, the world (and the works by which that world is made manifest) erupts continuously out of an irrepressible point of origin. An iridescent chaos, as Cézanne once put it: a place from which the virginity of the world might, once again, be experienced. An area that antecedes reference, coordinates, points of orientation, that refuses any form of pre-established measure in its protean capacity to generate—and perpetuate—all such measure.

The waves writhe. About the rims, shoulders, hips of so much earthenware, the pattern thrives in each of its fresh releases. As conceived by artisans, it celebrates the preconceptual. It speaks of a world that hasn't yet fallen under the dictates of human determinism. Spontaneous, convulsive, this original wave pattern, however, will adorn Ionico-Massalian pottery for a remarkably short period of time. Under the effects of an emergent humanism, the pattern itself will rapidly harden. Codified into bands of identical, oscillating units, it will vanish altogether as an expression of emergence. By the fifth century B.C., it appears as little more than a script confined to mechanical repetition. It has fallen victim, in short, to number.

This evolution followed that of philosophy itself. Within a half-century—from the time, that is, of Heraclitus and most of the pre-Socratics to that of Socrates—*rhitmos* would find itself redefined in an increasingly narrow manner. Plato himself qualified rhythm as "the order of movement" manifested, say, by a dancer in measured, predetermined intervals. One had already entered the reign of *metron*. From an elemental vision of emergence, notions of number, of discrete units of articulated time, increasingly predominated. The potter's hand could only follow. Indeed, in Henri Maldiney's words, "measure had introduced the idea of limit (*peras*) into the midst of the limitless (*apeiron*). Between these two extremes, the destiny of rhythm itself would unfold: would die, finally, from inertia, dissipation."[7] Would die, finally, with the Latin *cadare, cadentia*, the mechanical breath-fall of our own acquired notions of "cadence."

With the ossification of the wave pattern, we become witnesses to the cryptic birth of a certain technological ideation. Traveling from *Logos* to *Eidos*, we reach—in an amazingly brief period of time—the very thresholds of concept, an order of thought that no longer needs to acknowledge its own origins, inception, emergence. In recognizing no antecedent, it cannot, in turn, generate sequence, translate energy. Static, self-sufficing, it can do little more than replicate—*ex nihilo*—its own formulations.

How much of modern conceptual art today celebrates this very immobility, exults in its own truncated vision? "Sad," Schiller will warn Hegel, "the empire of concept: out of a thousand changing forms, it will create but one: destitute, empty."[8] We see it all too often in galleries; read it, over and over, in postmodernist journals; find ourselves increasingly exposed to an astonishingly similar, astonishingly rigid vision of existence. An art so deliberately sepulchral can only be, indeed, an end-art. Can only be, finally, a vain exercise in the service of a terminal aesthetics.

Here, though, we're not concerned with endings but beginnings: with that inaugural instant in Western civilization that would recognize itself not in its mirrors but its waves, in the irrepressible flow of an inexhaustible dynamic: that of Being. Vectorial by nature, it would express itself in a multitude of ways. The archaic wave pattern happens to be one such way. As a signature, it ripples freely across the flanks of so much salvaged terra-cotta in its own inimitable script. It speaks, as it goes, pure transmission.

How can we help but marvel, discovering one of those potsherds ourselves? At Saint Blaise, for instance, after the winter rains, a fragment may inch its way to the surface out of some excavated cross section. Examining the supple lash of its undulations whipping their way across this all-too-abbreviated fragment, we might find ourselves wondering what *is* it, exactly, if not current itself. If not the still-living filament to a lost luminosity. If not, indeed, the limpid inscription that has somehow survived (like Heraclitus's fragments) its vernal discourse. We might find ourselves asking these questions as we hold the potsherd between thumb and forefinger. Hold it like some kind of key. Hold it like some very particular kind of key to some very particular kind of door. The door, alas, has long since vanished.

Dum elephanti traiciuntur . . .
LIVY, *AB URBE CONDITA*

Tracking Hannibal 🖋

I

There's a word missing. And, without it, without that single, indispensable qualifier, we'll never be entirely free of guesswork, idle speculation, academic conjecture. I'm not referring, here, to some ontological puzzle touching on, say, the nature of existence, but the location of a particular event at the outset of the Second Punic War: namely, the exact point at which Hannibal crossed the Rhone. Does it really matter, though? Who in fact cares about an event so relatively minor within the entire breadth—unraveling—of history itself? Why should this particular moment in the late summer of 218 B.C. be the focal point of such lavish attention? Such meticulous, painstaking examination?

There's a word missing. And history, a system that tends toward closure, irrefutable fact, finds itself in this instance confronted by an omission, a lacuna. Finds its tightly woven fabric momentarily rent. It may well be the underlying cause, indeed, of so much obsessive attention, why innumerable hypotheses have been emitted in regard to Hannibal's exact point of crossing.

The lacuna in itself draws the scholar's curiosity with all the involuting magnetism of some low pressure zone, some cyclonic eye. For this tiny textual oversight, this minor omission in the running narrative of Hannibal's exploits, has generated an entire literature based on interpolation alone. History, we come to realize, has a horror of omissions. It comes rushing, each time, into its gaps, silences, hiatuses. Comes rushing with a scarcely concealed voracity.

From Narbonne to the Rhone crossing, Polybius is explicit: Hannibal's armies had marched one thousand *stadia* (approximately 185 kilometers) to reach the banks of the river. But which banks, exactly? We can be certain that he'd taken, in crossing Languedoc, the Via Iberia (later known as the Via Domitia, a Roman Praetorian route). Passing through the territory of the Volcae, whose capital was Nîmes—a final stage-point on the Via Iberia before the Rhone itself— he would normally have reached the crossing at a level with Beaucaire. But did he, in fact?

It's far easier to imagine Hannibal and his armies than to fix their exact location at any given point. Easier to imagine the clouds of late summer dust that must have arisen from the trampling of fifty thousand foot soldiers, nine thousand Numidian horsemen on horseback, an inexhaustible quantity of pack animals, not to mention the soft, waddling gait of thirty-seven mounted elephants, striking terror as they went into the heart of incredulous Gaul. As for Hannibal, his name alone—"By the Grace of the God Baal"—speaks eloquently enough. Riding one of those immense, ungainly creatures, one can readily imagine that twenty-six-year-old warrior—already considered a genius in the dark art of strategy—as if enlightened from within. We have Livy's account (drawn, no doubt, from some Carthaginian source) of Hannibal's dream: how, only months earlier, a youth of divine aspect (*iuuenem diuina specie*) had appeared to Hannibal in his sleep, sent by Jupiter himself to guide the young warlord on his march into Italy.[1] With Baal behind him and Jupiter—like a star—ahead, how could Hannibal help but feel enlightened, protected as he was by those invisible forces?

From the outset, he had three major material preoccupations. First he'd been obliged to bide his time, to camp with his immense armies in Cartagena (Carthago Novo), Spain, until the spring crops had been harvested and his troops adequately supplied with rations. This had meant delaying the entire campaign until late May at the earliest. Next came the Rhone crossing. At no point in his immensely perilous journey would his armies be more exposed, open to attack. In September, he knew, the Rhone's waterline would be at its lowest, and the river itself at its most amenable. No moment could be better chosen. Last came the greatest obstacle of all: the Alps, the imperious gateway onto the Italic plains and, ultimately, Rome itself. These, as Hannibal well knew, had to be crossed before the Pleiades had set in the western sky (*occidente iam sidere Vergiliarum*)[2]—before, that is, the first snows fell.

Considering the scale and daring of such an adventure, why should we—twenty-two hundred years later—confine ourselves to the petty details of one specific instance: those hypothetical crossing points in Hannibal's vast démarche? I find myself asking this question as I, too, enter the puzzle, following the banks of the Rhone this morning—geodetic survey maps in hand—traveling northward from the lowest conceivable crossing point, inspecting each alternative, each purported site, as I go. What, though, could anyone add to those endless pages of supposition already written, that endless catalog of postulates? I stare at the river, the perfectly flat, imperturbable slip of its pearl-grey waters, asking myself that very question. What's left to be determined?

The Greek historian, Polybius, is both our first and our most indispensable source of information. His *Historiae*, covering the full fifty-three-year span of the Second Punic War (beginning with its causes and concluding with Rome's total subjugation of the Carthaginian empire) was written only seventy years after Hannibal's astonishing blitzkrieg across Gaul. Drawing heavily on documented reports left by Hannibal's own historians, on eyewitness accounts, and on his own footwork (he would trace Hannibal's entire trajectory himself), Polybius was an utterly faithful, if somewhat verbose, chronicler of these events. Indeed, his own account often reads like an "engineer's report," as one modern historian put it.[3] Why, then, hasn't Polybius himself furnished us with the missing word, the long-vanished locative? Given his respect for painstaking accuracy, why didn't he fix the exact crossing point forever in his written *Historiae*? Polybius himself supplies us with an answer. In Book 3 he writes: " . . . in unknown regions, the enumeration of place names has, I feel, no more value than words devoid of all meaning, than a mere babble of sounds."[4] Writing in Greek for readers totally unfamiliar with the geography of those scarcely explored regions, Polybius simply deleted most place names altogether. Instead, he employed what might be called spatial indices: cardinal points to indicate direction, and either *stadia* (a unit of length) or marching days to indicate distance. Both, of course, could be readily comprehended by his Greek readers; his descriptions were totally exempt from meaningless toponym.

What, then, about the documented reports left by Hannibal's own historians, those who'd accompanied the warrior throughout the various stages of his vast expedition? Polybius himself had drawn freely from these Carthaginian sources and had even berated them in his *Historiae* for cluttering their own accounts with toponyms, those place names devoid of any significance whatsoever. One thinks especially of Silenus—one of seven known Carthaginian sources—who was not only Hannibal's personal historian but also a companion-in-arms in his march across Gaul. Certainly Silenus would have named the exact crossing point and the battle that immediately ensued. And, most certainly, he had. But along with the six others, Silenus's accounts have totally vanished. Nothing remains of their work except their names. History, here, has deprived us of everything but the vacuous signature of its historians.

Silence is a relative quality: there are degrees of silence just as there are degrees of sound. Here, for instance, with the loss of these seven contemporary eyewitness accounts, the silence of history itself has deepened, amplified. We've traced the event down to its most immediate, recorded sources and discovered that the sources themselves have disappeared. We have no choice but to move forward in time, to seek out classical historians who still happened to have access to those works, hoping, as we do, to detect some thin trickle of evidence.

Coelius Antipater, a Roman annalist working at about the same time as Polybius, compiled a monograph on the Second Punic War in seven consecutive volumes. Considered a highly reliable source by Valerius Maximus,[5] it must certainly have contained our missing word. But Coelius's monograph has, alas, vanished as well. Like the works of those Carthaginian historians, it too has entered a level of silence that we can only consider as absolute. Searching for a scrap of historical information, we've encountered nothing but deliberate deletion on Polybius's part and the successive effacement of recorded testimony owing to the barbarity or brute indifference of the Dark Ages that followed.

There remains Livy. Considered along with Tacitus and Sallust as one of Rome's greatest historians, Livy wrote an account of Hannibal's expedition in Book 21 of his vast, sweeping, eight-hundred-year *Ab urbe condita* (History of Rome). The pages of that book contain some of the most celebrated passages in all of Latin literature. They belong, indeed, more to literature than history, as Livy—with an aristocratic disdain for verifiable fact—worked his narrative to a high rhetorical polish. Drawing freely from not only Polybius and Coelius Antipater but also from the seven vanished Carthaginian histories, he conflated his materials into a single flowing narrative, a *flumen orationis* of his own. For all its beauty, however, it leaves us guessing. Rarely citing the names of his historical informants, Livy offers up a "cut-and-paste" version—as Sir Gavin de Beer put it—of Hannibal's great exploits.[6] We'll never know, of course, which parts originated where. With Livy, we're continuously at the mercy of amalgamated material and, inevitably, this material comes to contradict itself. Furthermore, if Polybius chose to delete place names in favor of spatial indicators (distance and direction), Livy did exactly the same, but for the sake of tribal territories. He located events in history according to whose territory in which they happened to occur. Hannibal crossed the Rhone, he tells us, in the land of the Volcae. Alas, the "land of the Volcae" designates an area far too extensive, lying on either side of the Rhone, to lend itself to anything more than exacerbated guesswork, shallow speculation.

There's a word missing: a single, precise, irrefutable place name. And, in its absence, the question itself remains posed—history itself suspended—over the geographical particulars of a few dusty, tumultuous days, twenty-two hundred years earlier.

Here I am, then, reading Polybius along the banks of the Rhone in my own rudimentary Greek, murmuring phrases to the waters before me, as if the waters themselves could be awakened from their somnolence, stirred—on syllables alone—from centuries of flat, placid self-absorption. I'm at Arles, this morning. Or, rather, at Fourques, facing Arles across the waters of the Rhone which are moving, here, at no less than two meters a second. A traditional crossing place since protohistoric times, Fourques-Arles represents the lowest—southernmost—point yet proposed as that of Hannibal's. In fact, in the absence of a single certifiable crossing, more than thirty carefully researched, thoroughly plausible locations have been proposed. From Seneca to Napoleon Bonaparte, the hypotheses abound. One of them, of course, is correct, for certainly Hannibal must have crossed somewhere. But where, exactly? *Grosso modo*, there are two schools of thought: that his crossing point was fairly close to the sea (thus, possibly, at Fourques-Arles) or that it was as far removed from the sea as Hannibal could reach within the allotted marching time. For the Carthaginian had to contend with not only a vast army of hostile Gauls, already massed on the opposite bank of the Rhone, but also a Roman consular force, led by Publius Cornelius Scipio, which was hard on his heels. If Polybius suggests, on three separate occasions, Hannibal's proximity to the sea throughout these events, he also tells us that Hannibal crossed the Rhone at a distance from the sea equivalent to "four marching days" (3.42.1). Here he enters into complete contradiction with himself and introduces one of the errors that will set historians astray for two millennia. Which of these two versions should we believe? Furthermore, when Polybius indicates "four marching days" from the sea, we have to ask ourselves, once again, from where? From Fos, the Roman Fossa Maritima, or some other coastal station, further to the west? As to the marching days themselves, how should we calculate that distance? Scipio's full-sized consular force, we know, moved at a rate of fifteen kilometers a day, whereas Xenophon indicated a rate of twenty-two kilometers a day for Cyrus's legions, and Caesar himself boasted of nothing less than twenty-seven kilometers a day in his own conquest of Gaul. Which of these distances, finally, constitutes a marching day in Polybian terms?

If the hypothesis of a crossing point somewhere near the sea (for example,

Fourques-Arles, or Beaucaire-Tarascon) has the advantage of a certain in-eluctability—these were traditional points of crossing, fully equipped with fer-ries, rafts, coracles—a point further to the north satisfies more fully the de-scriptions we have of Hannibal's immense strategic cunning. Livy clearly stipulates (21.31.2) that Hannibal, in removing himself as far as possible from the coastline, felt he might avert the Roman forces altogether. Even better, we have a single lapidary phrase from Zonaras: "Hannibal himself always avoided the obvious way."[7]

Whichever hypothesis we tend to support, we find ourselves confronted by inherent contradictions. The closer we read—the more exacting our exami-nation—the more enigmatic and ambivalent our findings. For each grounded argument, there's a counterargument; for each proof, a refutation. Have we entered, here, some kind of parable, some esoteric object lesson, say, on the nature of knowledge itself?

What, in material terms, am I looking for this morning? First, an area along the west bank of the Rhone broad enough to allow an army of sixty thousand men to mass in martial order and prepare their attack upon the facing bank. In short, a vast staging area.[8] Part of that preparation would include the felling of trees (poplars mostly) for the sake of constructing, in haste, the rafts, barks, and pontoons necessary for that crossing. Next, there'd have to be a relatively flat plain *en face*. Hannibal wouldn't have given his enemies the advantage of a natural shelter behind rocks, ledges, hillsides; he would have forced them down onto the same merciless level as himself: that of the riverbank. He would have chosen, quite deliberately, his own beachhead.

Polybius tells us that several days before the attack, Hannibal (as the in-ventor, most likely, of commando tactics) sent Hannon, one of his most trusted generals, two hundred *stadia* (thirty-seven kilometers) northward with a contingent of troops. There, where an island lay in the midst of the Rhone, the waters would be at their widest, and, consequently, their most shallow. Hannon's troops could swim across at this very point, floating on their wooden shields, dragging behind them bloated goatskins laden with their impedimenta.

I needed to locate an island, then, situated a certain number of kilometers north of two facing plains: one on which Hannibal's troops might have been deployed; the other on which he would have engaged the Gauls in combat. Altogether, these three locations constituted the geographical determinants by which I might postulate Hannibal's crossing point. Furthermore, there was a fourth factor: Hannon, having crossed the Rhone and landed on the opposite bank with his swift, lightly equipped, elite corps, sent Hannibal a smoke signal (*ex loco edito fumo*, Livy 21.27.7) from a hill just behind or beside the battle site itself. He did so, according to Polybius (3.43.1), only a moment before daybreak. With that signal, the battle commenced. In a conjoined maneuver, Hannon took the Gauls by surprise from the rear as Hannibal, in a frontal attack, led a first wave of light cavalry across the river. By nightfall, we read, Hannibal's victory would be assured.[9] Firmly established on the east bank of the Rhone, nothing but the Alps would stand between the Carthaginian and his ultimate ambition: Rome itself.

Along with my three other determinants, I had to locate the hill "just behind or beside the battle site." All four of these locations had to coincide with one another, mesh topologically. So, starting at Fourques, I set out. Carrying battered Loeb Classic editions of both Polybius and Livy, a sheath of notes I'd taken from the works of the specialists, and a complete set of geodetic survey maps covering the lower reaches of the Rhone valley, I made my way gradually northward. I was delayed at the outset by a ground fog that kept me from taking clear cross-river sightings, but a mistral arose by nine that morning which virtually delivered the landscape, rendered it crystalline. Along with the mistral came the sun. A clear, mid-winter day in Provence now lay before me in which to visit a whole host of proposed sites, to verify or dismiss each of them as I went.

From the survey maps alone, I was well aware that any number of islands lay in the middle of the Rhone; several of them could easily qualify as the one that Hannon crossed with his small troop of commandos. I could readily discern, for instance, the Ile de la Barthelasse off Avignon, the Ile de la Piboulette between Ardoise and Caderousse, and—further to the north—the Ile du Malatras in the vicinity of Pont-Saint-Esprit. Indeed, each of these islands has been proposed as Hannon's by a number of specialists over the years. But did any of them lie thirty-seven kilometers north of a pair of facing plains? And, if so, did the plain on the opposite (eastern) bank possess an overhanging ledge or hillock from which a smoke signal—undetected by an enemy, just beneath— might have been lit?

After traveling over ninety kilometers northward to Pont-Saint-Esprit, inspecting each postulated site, triangulating, as I went, between the various topological determinants involved, I came, at last, to an irrefutable conclusion. *None* of the sites proposed or suggested corresponded with the existent physical realities. If nearly all of them satisfied three of the given characteristics, not one of them coincided with all four. If, for instance, I found a number of matching plains, several of which lay thirty-seven kilometers south of an island, I never found the rock overhang or hillock befitting. Or, if I did, I wouldn't find the island or the plains in their appropriate contextual positions. There was always a piece missing in this four-piece puzzle I was playing with history. Or was history, in fact, playing with me? Laying out false directives for the sake of concealing some cherished moment all the more consummately?

I would only belabor the issue by extending my area of research into the Alps themselves. For there, the same textual problems exist, but multiplied a thousandfold. Perhaps no single event in Roman antiquity has given rise to so much controversy as the exact passage Hannibal took in crossing the Alps. Be it the Rhone or the Alps, however, it's curious, I find, that each of these unspecified points involves passage. Each involves a single, perilous, all-determinate moment of territorial penetration in which the Carthaginian entered—forced his entry—into an entirely new region. Why, then, have these points, so crucial in themselves, gone unnamed? Even Livy, writing only a century and a half after Hannibal's passage, remarked that there existed amongst his contemporaries serious doubt as to which Alpine pass Hannibal actually took (*ambigi quanam Alpes [Hannibal] transierit*, 21.38.6). Dennis Proctor, in his brilliant study, "Hannibal's March in History," refers to the silence of those contemporaries. "Varro, Pompey, Strabo, Cornelius Nepos, Appian, and Ammianus Marcellinus," he writes, "apart from Polybius and Livy themselves, all mentioned Hannibal's pass in one context or another, but not one of them gave it a name or referred to it in any other way than as Hannibal's pass. . . ."[10]

This curious lacuna generated doubt, confusion, or a certain embarrassed silence on the part of those early historians. Even more it created, with time, a plethora of speculation. A first monograph on the subject appeared in 1535, followed, in each century, by hundreds of refutations, correctives, counterproposals. Scaliger, Casaubon, Gibbon, Napoleon, and Mommsen, among many others, would make their contributions. None, however, would entirely concur. Even today, come late October and the proverbial "setting of the Pleiades"—the moment, that is, of Hannibal's crossing—the Alpine passes are visited by a seemingly inexhaustible number of prospecting Hannibal scholars. What do they expect to find at those altitudes? Having already compared the irreconcilable textual differences between Polybius and Livy, they'll attempt to determine the material conditions prevalent, at that moment, at some specific col. Measuring, say, the exact angle of each feasible slope or the "adhesion potential" of a hypothetical four-ton elephant on the freshly fallen snows of that slope, they'll arrive, quite often, at some entirely new hypothesis of their own. Questioning forest rangers, chamois hunters, road maintenance workers, priests in their mountain parishes, they'll come to ever new conclusions. Given that there exists more than forty negotiable passes between the Great Saint Bernard and the Col de Larche (the passes themselves ranging from mule trails to tarred roads), and that most of those passes possess a variety of approach routes of their own, the possibilities are virtually limitless. So, too, is the number of hypotheses advanced.

There is, quite clearly, a word missing. Or, more exactly, *words* missing from the pages of those first, founding, historical documents. Here, as elsewhere, history is riddled. Instead of a locative, we discover, in its place, a lacuna. Where an all-determinate event in history occurred, we're given, within the running fabric of those earliest narratives, a deliberate deletion in one case, a careless oversight in another, a succession of eloquent silences in yet others. Why, then, haven't historians simply accepted the good advice, say, of Marc Bloch? "Having explored every given possibility," he suggested, "there comes a time when a scholar's greatest duty is simply to confess ignorance and admit to it openly."[11] Why, to the contrary, this insistence? Why have an endless number of trekkers tested one col after another, written—on speculation alone—an incalculable quantity of monographs touching on Hannibal's "true Alpine pass," or spent long days, as I have done, attempting to determine the exact point at which the Carthaginian crossed the Rhone?

"The problem, here," as Ulrich Kahrstedt, a German classicist, astutely observed, "isn't topographical so much as historico-literary."[12] And, as I've already suggested, the nature of history is one that tends toward closure, conclusiveness, a seamless weave of sequential events. Most of the time, we feel ourselves an integral part of that continuum. That unbroken pattern. When, however, that pattern undergoes rupture, suffers hiatus for even the briefest instant, a certain intellectual anxiety results. Call it a zone of mnemonic instability. The void, we feel, must be filled; the lacuna, rectified. We come rushing into those areas of omission with a fervor bordering on the obsessional. Like bees, their metabolism stimulated at a certain given temperature, we swarm to the indeterminate: attempt to enter the very vocables that history, inadvertently or not, has left open.

Hannibal was fortunate, I find myself thinking. It's already late afternoon, now, as I gaze across the Rhone at one of the last hypothetical crossing points and muse on that doomed twenty-six-year-old warrior. On the opposite side, light is striking the ruins of a medieval watchtower—this very instant—a rich, carmine red. Yes, Hannibal was fortunate, for he'd managed to escape—at certain critical moments—his own historians. Those moments, and most notably the two perilous episodes involving passage, penetration, and the conquest of an entirely new territory, remain as if suspended, abeyant. They belong to a blank language. An empty script. Historians will go on postulating, speculating, demolishing one thesis for the sake of advancing another. It won't matter. As I watch the channel buoys bob in the draft of that deep, unremitting current, I'm fully convinced that that language will remain blank; that script, empty. The book, complete with the inaudible trumpeting of its thirty-seven volatilized elephants, will lie forever open.

for Jérôme Rimbert

What the Thunder Said ⪡

Fulgur Conditum, the inscription reads: [Here] lightning [has been] buried. Altars, stone tablets, commemorative markers bearing that same terse inscription are still occasionally discovered on the barren, wind-blown plateaus of rural Provence. For wherever lightning strikes (drawn, no doubt, by a high level of electromagnetism) there's a likelihood that the Gallo-Roman rites of thunderbolt burial were once practiced. Considered sacred (*sacer*), as the very signature of Jupiter himself, lightning was "interred" at the exact point at which it fell. Along with the lightning bolt were buried whatever bits of wood, roof tile, etc. (*dispersos fulminus ignes*), that might have burnt in its passage. A small cylindrical retaining wall (a *puteal*) was erected around the point itself, the above-mentioned epigraph affixed, an animal (usually a sheep, a *bidens*) sacrificed in expiation, and the enclosed ground consecrated by an officiating priest. This priest, a *fulguratore*, was fully initiated in the art of lightning worship. The ritual itself was immediately followed by an interdiction:

Gallo-Roman altar bearing the inscription Fulgur
conditum: *Here lightning has been buried.*
Photo by the author.

no one, henceforth, could approach the consecrated area nor gaze upon it from a distance. For it had now become the inviolable territory of Iupiter Fulgerator himself.

The Roman poet, Lucan, has left eloquent testimony to such a ritual. Arrus, we may assume, was the officiating priest in this particular instance:

Arrus gathered together the lightning's scattered fires,
Buried them in murmuring dark formula,
Placing the site, thereby, under divine protection.[1]

These ceremonies, or *exhortio*, were aimed at eliminating any destructive forces still inherent within the thunderbolt itself, while preserving its sacred character in the shafts of the consecrated earthen wells. Lightning, as divine manifestation, was thus secured within a context of strict sacerdotal observation: its holy fires were ritually "housed."

From classical sources, we have abundant evidence of the awe that these forked fires once inspired. Plutarch, for instance, tells us that whoever happened to be touched by lightning was considered invested with divine powers, whereas anyone slain by one of its jagged bolts was deemed equal to the gods themselves.[2] Furthermore, it was believed that the bodies of those struck dead by lightning weren't subject to decomposition, for their innards had been embalmed by nothing less than celestial fire.

Ultimate nexus between heaven and earth, the lightning bolt has a mythopoeic history that can be traced as far back as the Assyrians. They considered its sacred fire not so much an attribute of their divinity, Bin, as his very manifestation. The same would hold true for the Phoenicians, the Egyptians, and the Cypriots. It is not until the cult of lightning reaches Greece, transmitted no doubt by those pre-Hellenic people, the Palasgi, that the lightning bolt as divine manifestation becomes *sema*, sign, the personal attribute of an otherwise invisible deity whose reign would now extend over all atmospheric phenomena: Zeus Keraunos.

Undergoing continual changes within Greece itself, lightning worship would reach Rome through the mediation—call it the divinatory agency—of

Etruscan priests. Indeed, these priests, the *fulguratores*, armed with their notorious *libri fulgurales* (oracular books in which questions were posed in archaic Latin and answered by these mediators in Etruscan) dominated the Roman cult of lightning worship until the end of the Roman Empire. Even the original Italic figure of Jupiter, thunderbolt in hand, underwent a certain "Etruscification." Originally considered a sky spirit (a *numen*) in archaic Roman mythology, he takes on the epithets *optimus* and *maximus* under the spiritual tutelage of these mediating Etruscan haruspices. A magnificent temple in his honor was erected on the pinnacle of the Capitoline, commissioned, no doubt, by Tarquinius Priscus and Tarquinius Superbus, the semilegendary twin kings of Rome, reputedly Etruscan themselves. There, the effigy of Jupiter was flanked on either side by the goddesses Juno and Minerva, forming a triadic divinity thoroughly Greco-Etruscan in inspiration.

Whether we're considering this original Italic spirit reigning over all things atmospheric, his elevation to Jupiter Optimus Maximus upon the pantheon of the Capitoline or, much later, one of his Gallo-Roman variants here in the distant hills of Provence, we discover that Jupiter may be identified by two opposing characteristics. The first is evident enough: Jupiter, unfailingly, bears the thunderbolt. Be he Iupiter Fulminator casting the bolt itself, Iupiter Fulgerator revealing himself in its very flash, or Iupiter Tonans declaring his presence in a roll of thunder, he wields, in every instance, that celestial fire. There's a second characteristic, however, that lies as if secreted within the first. As with virtually all archaic representations, characteristics invariably come paired in antithetical sets. The evident conceals the covert, the manifest, the obscure. Modern studies in ethnology, linguistics, and other related disciplines have made us increasingly aware of this particular phenomenon. In 1910 Freud was already writing in regard to words: " . . . it is in the 'oldest roots' that the antithetical double meaning is to be observed. Then in the further course of its development, these double meanings [tend to] disappear." Same, too, Freud continues, with the "archaic character of thought-expression [found] in dreams."[3] In tracing the etymological origin of a particular word ourselves, how often we'll fall upon one of these antitheses, as if the word itself was embodying, at its very inception, a paired set of opposing signifiers.

In a relatively rare epigrammatic discovery, a Gallo-Roman altar unearthed near Aix-en-Provence bears the inscription *Iovo Frugifero*: that is, Iupiter Frugifer. Signifying fertility, fecundity, the instigator of harvest, it would appear at first as an epithet signifying an entirely different divinity. How do we get from *Fulgerator* to *Frugifer*, from Jupiter wielding lightning, to Jupiter bearing fruit? Obviously, lightning brings rain, and rain, fertility, but how do these two separate, sequential events find shelter within a single all-encompassing vocable? The entire question lies there.

Turning to Roman folk mythology for support, we learn that Jupiter, as the supreme divinity, was celebrated throughout the year not only as master of lightning but also as protector of crops.[4] The *Feriae Jovis*, festivities dedicated to Jupiter, honored the guardian of the vineyard, the grape harvest, and the winepress. From the *Vinalia priora* in spring to the *Meditrinalia* in autumn, Jupiter was invoked at every crucial moment in the vintner's calendar. It was unto Jupiter that wine was offered, rendered, consumed. Other *Feriae Jovis* that might be mentioned in regard to Jupiter's "parallel identity" include the *Robigalia* and *Floralia* of spring. Both of these festivities served as propitiatory rites in favor of the young grain: the first as a protection against blight, the second as a stimulation or encouragement to the kernel itself. Here, once again, Jupiter, master of the heavens, was the ultimate mediator in matters strictly terrestrial, agrarian.

A sculpture discovered in one of Rome's distant colonies in North Africa (near present-day Zaghouan, Tunisia) depicts Jupiter bearing in one hand the inevitable thunderbolt, while in the other, instead of the traditional scepter, a cornucopia filled with fruit. With this sculpture, we have a perfect iconographic representation of the god in all his archaic ambivalence. Both fulguration and fructification find themselves depicted within a single homogenous statement. Together, one and the other are brought to coalesce.

How does Jupiter accumulate, or should we say incorporate, such powers? A line from Pliny's *Naturalis historia* might help elucidate the deliberately maintained ambivalence of these twin attributes. Pliny, describing the *libri fulgurales*, writes that the Etruscan *fulguratores*, charged with all matters pertaining to lightning—be it its observation (*observatio*), interpretation (*interpretatio*) or propitiation (*exhortio*)—believed that the lightning bolt itself penetrated the earth to a depth of five feet.[5] This remark is not as insignificant as it may appear. For it tells us that lightning, in the eyes of those mediating Etruscan priests, didn't simply strike and consequently ground itself against the surface of the earth: it actually entered, penetrated the earth as its recipient body. In the language of Eliade, we're in the presence, here, of an "antique hierogamy." Between Jupiter, the "Celestial Thunder God," and Jupiter, the "Bearer of Fruit," we might well be witnesses to that archaic ambivalence mentioned above—that deep-seated androgyny—wherein the god incorporates the qualities of both fructifier and fructified, inseminator and inseminated. Soon, these very qualities will undergo separation. Jupiter will retain his thunderbolt, but an ubiquitous earth-mother will come to reassert her place as the bearer of all earthly goods. Soon, each will be assigned separate, complementary roles in this evolving mythology, this coital enactment "indispensable to the very energies which assure bio-cosmic fertility."[6]

Discussing one of the many engraved inscriptions bearing the words *Fulgur Conditum*, the late Marcel Leglay made the following pertinent remark:

> If lightning is buried with so much care and precaution, its sacred stones deposited beneath an earthen mound that's ringed, in turn, by a boundary wall, and the *locus* altogether consecrated, is it only for the sake of self-protection? For neutralizing the effects of the lightning bolt? For observing, in short, a taboo? It wouldn't seem so. In my opinion, it's more for the sake of preserving, preciously safeguarding *in situ*, the source of both the inception and diffusion of that terrestrial fire. The source, indeed, of life itself.[7]

More than fortuitous points of momentary impact, these "wells" of celestial penetration needed to be circumscribed, the divine fire that they'd introduced *retained* within the entrails of the earth itself. Out of this encounter, all things living, ineluctably, would spring.

By way of illustration, we only need examine a relatively nondescript limestone altar discovered in the region of Nîmes. Here, the two-word inscription, rather than reading *Fulgur Conditum*, commemorates in stately Roman capitals *Terra Matri*. Just over this inscription lies engraved the truncated half of a wheel. The emblem of the Celtic god Taranis, this wheel designates thunder. As Jupiter's Celtic counterpart within that widespread family of Indo-European divinities, Taranis's attribute isn't the lightning bolt, but its sonorous aftermath, the hollow thunderclap. The wheel, in the roar of its iron hoop over cobbles, serves as a perfect mimetic signifier. Even Taranis's name, drawn directly from the Celtic root, *tarans*, designates nothing less than thunder itself. Together, we have, reunited in that simple, somewhat austere altar, the two fundamental protagonists in this cosmic drama: heaven and earth; fire and the ground it fecundates; celestial father and the now distinct terrestrial mother, represented in pure symbiosis.

*The wheel, attribute of the Celtic thunder god
Taranis, represented in direct relation to Mother
Earth, Terra Matri. Photo by the author.*

Dedicated to those two indissociable forces, the altar helps clarify the meaning of the Gallo-Roman cult of lightning worship. Clearly enough, the burial of that celestial fire was a means of conserving its procreant energies within the sacred interiors of the earth itself. In a dialectic of opposites, the altar celebrates the indispensability of each within the cosmic contextuality of both. Furthermore, it tells us, in no more than two words and a single icono-graphic device, exactly "what the thunder said."

In the high barren wastelands of the Alpes-de-Haute-Provence, lightning con-tinues to fall in the same areas where Gallo-Roman *Fulgur Conditum* inscrip-tions are still occasionally discovered. These discoveries aren't fortuitous. De-spite the popular dictum, lightning not only strikes twice, it strikes the same location repeatedly if that location happens to be, as here, on raised ground and rich in ferromagnetic deposits. Lightning, in these parts, falls frequently. And if, in the past two thousand years, its "entry" no longer receives the kind of consecration it once enjoyed from the hands of officiating *fulguratores*, we might consider, at least, yet another form of reception. For lightning, the sheer, unmitigated experience of lightning, continues to provoke in the subsoils of our own psyche an inexpungible sense of awe. Devoid now of all ritual, the sublimating effects of all mythopoeic projection, it continues to arouse, nonetheless, the kind of dread and reverence that's always been its due. Am-bivalent, provocative, it goes on striking at our deepest, most dormant levels of consciousness. Yes, lightning keeps falling. And its fires, perforating the frail armor of late postmodern rationality, continue to instill, enlighten. Continue to nourish the most fertile regions of our imagination with so many succes-sive bolts of pure, unprogrammed luminosity.

for Tina Jolas

Aeria the Evanescent ✍

There's a lost city in Provence named after air itself: Aeria. A *polis* to the Greeks, a *civitas* to the Romans, Aeria must have been of considerable size and located at an exceptional altitude. The Greek geographer, Strabo, mentioned it along with Avignon and Orange and described the site as something "altogether aerial, constructed on a raised promontory of its own."[1]

How could such a sizable, protohistoric city (it was founded, apparently, by the Celts) simply disappear, one wonders? For Provençal historians it represents a major enigma and a source of unending polemic. Scarcely a year passes without the publication of some article, pamphlet, or documented field report offering "at long last, irrefutable evidence" as to Aeria's exact location. In reading these reports one comes to feel that Aeria might have been anywhere, everywhere, nowhere at once.[2] There's hardly a single raised, windblown plateau evincing the least Iron Age vestige that hasn't been identified as that of the lost city. I have read over fifty such reports written in the past two centuries and have managed to visit a considerable number of the sites proposed. The results, for the most part, have proved disappointing. Few of the purported "Aerias" even begin to fit the descriptions we've inherited from classical sources. What's more, it's the sources themselves that have been largely responsible for so much idle speculation. Brief, elusive, and highly ambivalent in their own right, they've undergone endless alterations at the hands of successive, often careless, medieval copyists. What, indeed, can they tell us today? Without falling into idle speculations of our own, what can we draw from these materials with any certitude whatsoever? How, in short, can we ourselves come to locate the City of Air?

We learn from Strabo that it lay somewhere between two rivers: the Durance to the south and the Isère to the north. A third river, the Rhone, would have constituted its furthest possible reach westward, while the Alpine foothills that of its potential limits eastward. Thus we can determine that this lost city lay within an area of somewhat less than a thousand square kilometers. We can reduce this figure even further: Aeria, according to Apollodorus, was Celtic,[3] and lay, in Strabo's words, within the confederated land of the Cavares.[4] These people occupied the fertile plains of the Rhone valley and its adjacent plateaus to the east. Rising up over those plains, Aeria must have been visible from a considerable distance and been immensely impressive for travelers such as the Greek chronicler Artemidorus. His mention of Aeria towards the end of the second century B.C. constitutes (along with Apollodorus's remark that Aeria was Celtic) our first topographical source. What else can be said with any certitude? We can safely postulate that Aeria lay somewhere north of Avignon and Orange, the two cities with which it is associated in Strabo's *Geographica*. Strabo almost certainly named these three cities in geographical order: from Avignon in the south to Aeria in the north. Beyond Aeria, he tells us, begins a wooded region, rife with narrow mountain passes. This region extends the length of a full day's march (approximately thirty kilometers) to a town called Durio. Of Durio, however, we know absolutely nothing. Nor can we begin to speculate on the identity of the two rivers which, according to Strabo, circumscribed Durio before converging in a single current towards the Rhone itself.

From Durio onward, we've gone thoroughly astray. The location of the town, of the two all-determinate rivers within a shifting landscape of textual incertitude has left us totally at the mercy of hypotheses. Even reduced, now, to an area of less than three hundred square kilometers, we have any number of perched Iron Age *oppida* from which to choose. Some, of course, can be quickly dismissed because of their insufficient altitude; others, because their table-top summits could scarcely have enclosed a full protohistoric city; yet others, because their profile—even if raised, massive, commanding— couldn't possibly have laid within sight of a major Greek trade route such as Artemidorus must have taken, traveling northward from Marseilles to Lyon.

We've narrowed our possibilities, however; we've reduced our area of prospection to a relatively narrow band of earth running approximately parallel to the left bank of the Rhone and in a region somewhat to the north of Orange. Within this area, several protohistoric sites have been proposed. One of them, the *oppidum* of Barri, has received particular attention recently from some of Provence's most respected historians. Lying just north of the market town of Bollène, itself traversed by the Lez (potentially one of the two tributaries mentioned by Strabo), the *oppidum* satisfies a number of conditions that could eventually lead to its identification as Aeria. Rising in an abrupt, vertical cliff over the plains, it commands a spectacular view of the Rhone valley beyond, as well as a controlling position over the ancient Greek trade route just beneath. Vast, rich in natural springs, and abounding in late Iron Age vestige, the site itself is eminently aerial. Wind-struck, it sits on its raised limestone podium, a good deal closer to the sky above than to the earth below.

A number of counterarguments, however, have come to weaken such an attribution. Despite a maximal altitude of 312 meters, the *oppidum* itself only rises, in fact, 200 meters over the plains. Would this difference in altitude have been sufficient to support the epithet *aerial?* Even more troubling, why would an entire city, a *polis*, have been located so close to yet another (in this instance, Orange)? Only twenty kilometers separate the two. In classical times, cities couldn't survive without an outlying *pagus* or canton, a richly cultivated farmland proportionate to the city's population. In this case, the *pagus* of one would have encroached on that of the other, and their respective sources of sustenance would have been inevitably compromised. What's more, the Celts traditionally founded their cities equidistant from one another. Indeed, the map of Celtic Gaul reads like a continuous network of evenly distributed communities often called, significantly enough, Médiolanum, "The City in the Middle." Here again, the *oppidum* of Barri is far too close to Orange to satisfy the conditions for such a practice of spatial distribution. Added to this, it must be noted that the *oppidum* isn't located in the territory of the Cavares, as Strabo specified, but that of the neighboring Tricastini.

Where are we then? Even if we've managed to reduce considerably the number of square kilometers in which Aeria might potentially be located, we're still adrift among hypotheses. Any number of perched, wind-struck *oppida* could still satisfy our altogether vague descriptions. As for myself, I've often wondered whether I've been searching, all the while, for a *location* or a *locution*: whether, that is, I've been looking for a place, an emplacement, a specific irrefutable *locus* or—to the contrary—for a word. For a word that would designate, certainly, such a place, but only in the buoyancy, the effervescence of its own iteration. A word that might invoke, within its very vocable, so much stonework and quicklime and smoldering hearth. One, in short, that might incorporate—in its atmospheric particles—an all-impacted, earthbound existence.

Aeria, the Aerial, the City of Air. It would be a sterile exercise in academic philology to speculate on whether the founding radical, *aer*, originated in Celtic or Greek. Both languages, having common Indo-European origins, shared approximately the same signifier. It would be safe to assume, however, that the toponym itself arose out of the Celtic and underwent, as an adjective feminized to agree with its substantive, *polis*, a certain Hellenization. As an adjective we find it frequently employed in Greek literature. It appears in Aeschylus's *Suppliants*, for example, or in its Ionic variant, *erea*, in Apollonius Rhodius's *Argonautica*. As toponym, however, it vanished from usage at exactly the same period as the *topos* it designated. As ever, the two—*topos* and toponym—would undergo a single inseparable fate. Neither Caesar nor Livy, for instance, mention Aeria in their descriptions of Gaul. If Pliny happens to include it in his list of Gallo-Roman communities within the recently established Provincia, he does so in qualifying the city an *oppidum latinum*.[5] The term itself suggests that the raised Celtic stronghold had undergone pacification, subjugation: had found itself reduced to a protectorate under the all-powerful *pax romana*. Soon after, the toponym vanished altogether from contemporary historical record. Neither Mela in the first century A.D. nor Ptolemy in the second include it in the comprehensive geographies that each compiled.

Other towns in Provincia would vanish as well. Of the thirty that Pliny listed, eight would leave nothing more than a name totally detached, now, from any verifiable location. Among those vanished communities, though, only Aeria would have qualified as *polis, civitas*: a city, opposed to a *vicus,* or simple township. Far more pertinent, only Aeria could lay claim to such an immensely evocative, if evanescent toponym. For it's the place name alone that draws us, over and over, onto the raised plateaus of Rhodian Provence, that keeps us searching in one site after another for the irrefutable evidence of some stray inscription, some carved, all-confirming epigraph. Who, after all, wouldn't wish to discover the City of Air? For centuries, erudites, country priests, local aristocrats, or simple curiosity-seekers have combed the region looking for that conclusive artifact wherein place (topographical), place name (toponymical) and vestige (archeological) would perfectly coincide. Many cried out success far too early. Writing in 1914, Alexandre Chevalier would claim that "After so many centuries of vain research and laborious investigation, History [*sic*] at long last has rediscovered the Antique City whose very existence had begun slipping into pure indifference."[6] Far more perspicacious, the German prehistorian Ernest Herzog would write, "*suum quisque locum invenit.*"[7] Herzog was suggesting, not without malice, that Aeria could be located anywhere one wished.

There's a danger, of course, in mystifying Aeria, in attributing hierographic powers to its place name. For certainly, it not only existed within a certain ascribable area, it left vestiges eloquent enough to allow for its eventual identification. In the meanwhile, however, its vocable continues to intrigue. For Aeria seems to exist free of the very floors and crypts and quarried vaults in which it once was rooted. In an age of reductive analysis and infallible detection, it continues to resist any classification whatsoever. Doing so, the very name of this elevated, windblown city exercises—we readily admit—a singular fascination. There's safety, we can't help feeling, in its indeterminate status. Its three weightless syllables have somehow managed to escape (for the moment, at least) any ultimate attribution. Buoyant, suspended, eminently diffuse, the vocable alone, in eluding us, justifies our fascination. Escaping our own stultifying structures, it gives the imagination a late place in which to muse, meditate, linger, if for no more—indeed—than a passing moment.

Votive Mirrors

The mirror itself was scarcely wider than an eye. Thirty millimeters in diameter, its reflection would have probably included, at its very edges, the line of a cheekbone just beneath, and the floating arch of an eyebrow just over. Within the mirror, we can only imagine, the eye must have come to gaze at its own wobbling likeness. There, undoubtedly, it would have paused, lingered. Around it, on the surrounding lead frame, ran the uninterrupted garland of a propitiatory inscription. For the mirror, the reflected eye and the metallic frame (bearing as it did this running inscription) constituted a sacred offering. Indeed, several of the inscribed mirrors thus far discovered in southern Gaul (essentially in the lower Rhone valley) bear a full votive inscription to a Greek divinity. They're dedicated either to Aphrodite, the goddess of love, or Selene, the goddess of the moon. Together, these two figures reigned over the world of love in each of its multiple aspects, be it erotic, sentimental, magical, or—in Selene's case—propagative.

0   2 cm

Frame of a votive mirror dedicated to Aphrodite.
Courtesy Guy Barruol.

We have, then, in concentric order, the eye, its reflection floating in the laminal disk of a glass mirror (one of the first of its kind), and the lead frame itself. The latter, square in outline, encased the pure circle of the mirror. Mirror—and reflection—have long since vanished, of course. We're dealing, after all, with evanescent materials dating from late antiquity: from, that is, the beginning of the second century to the end of the fourth. Nonetheless, minuscule bits of mirror have been detected still wedged between the narrow lead furrows of the frames. This "vitreous debris" has allowed specialists to determine the width of the glass itself (0.5mm in most cases), the method of its fabrication, and the all-essential undercoat it once received, be it lead, silver, or, occasionally, gold. Above and beyond these considerations, however, their attention has focused almost exclusively on the frames. For it's the lead frames themselves that have offered up such a wealth of information. Thanks to the inscriptions alone, the relationship between dedicator and dedicatee, votary and the object of devotion, can at last be determined. Nearly two thousand years after the fact, something as ephemeral as an individual's quivering reflection in a looking glass can now be interpreted in terms of a lost reciprocity. These were offerings, after all, to one of two specific divinities. As such, they initiated, if not a dialogue, a dialectic between an individual (the votary) and an otherwise invisible entity. Vestiges of a rural and, most certainly, popular tradition, they might be read today as elucidating artifacts.

Votive mirrors existed throughout antiquity. In fact, they're probably as old as mirrors themselves. Poured in bronze, at first, and polished on one side to a high reflective luster, they were far too hard for anything more than the simplest, tool-scratched inscription. Even uninscribed, however, we may assume that they already served as votive offerings to those same two divinities. Traditionally, Selene and Aphrodite were as much recipients of mirrors (as well as rings, earrings, bracelets) as, say, Demeter, goddess of crops, was of miniature metallic hoes, sickles, plowshares. These offerings were all part of what historians have called a "votive contract." Basically, this "contract" functioned in one of two ways: either to invoke the favor of a god or goddess (thus, as a votive instrument), or to thank a god or goddess for a favor rendered (functioning as an ex-voto or acquittance). In both cases, the object, whether mirror or not, served as a token of exchange between a mortal and an immortal.

"I'm giving you this," it suggested, "that you might grant me that." Or, in the latter case, "since you've granted me that, here, take this as a measure of my everlasting gratitude."

With the advent of blown glass in the first century A.D. came the earliest reflecting lenses, no bigger than monocles, such as those encased within these inscribed lead medallions. Whether they evolved into votive objects from women's cosmetic impedimenta (indirectly, that is) or, to the contrary, were especially designed as amulets to serve magical purposes, we may be certain that they belonged entirely to the domain of women. What's more, they were offered by these very women to female deities. We know, for instance, from references to a lost poem by Pindar, that women in love made offerings to Selene, the moon goddess, whereas men in love made offerings to her brother, Helios, the sun god.[1]

Three of the ten votive mirrors dedicated to either of the two goddesses still bear, in abbreviated Greek characters, a full dedicatory inscription. The same maker's name, Q. Licinios Touteinos, figures in each instance, as does the mirror's place of manufacture: Arelate (Arles). We can assume that this artisan was a lead smith (*plumbarius*) and most probably a mirror maker (*specularius*) as well. We may even consider the possibility that he was an initiate, a priest of sorts, in the mysteries of this amatory cult. Beyond that, however, it would be a serious mistake to confound his name with that of the votary. For the latter's name, unlike the artisan's, is never mentioned. Nor is the name of her beloved. We may infer, however, that the names of both votary and beloved need not have been named, for in the goddess's omniscience (be she Aphrodite or Selene) the names of her immediate subjects were already known, familiar, sympathetically perceived.

The fact that not only the goddesses but also the language employed in these votive inscriptions happen to be Greek requires a word of explanation. Writes the historian Guy Barruol: "With the use of a foreign language, familiar to only an intellectual elite in the lower valley of the Rhone but most certainly incomprehensible, thus alien, to the average devotee in the Gallic countryside, we might attribute an added power in the use of these objects, richly endowed with magic properties."[2] The use of Greek, in short, added strangeness, mystery, a deliberately orchestrated "otherness" to these votive inscriptions. Barruol goes on to tell us that, in the second and third centuries A.D., a resurgence in both magical and astrological practices, clearly originating in the Near East, made itself felt throughout southern Gaul. He suggests that a certain "religious syncretism" might have existed between Provincia itself and those distant, still Hellenized encampments far to the east. There, the wives of Roman legionnaires might well have assimilated some of the esoteric practices still observed in those parts and, upon arriving in their recently allotted homelands in southern Gaul, introduced those very practices, still Hellenized, into local forms of worship. As a working hypothesis, this mode of transmission is perfectly plausible. Then, too, it has the consistency of rendering the entire cult—from the ritual itself to its sociocultural dissemination—exclusively female.

Before closing, we might consider the mirrors themselves in yet another light. Aside from being the objects of a rigorous metaphysical barter—the tokens of exchange between a particular votary and her invoked divinity—we might see in their ritual use something far more personal, inclusive, reciprocal. For the exchange implied a communication of sorts. More than simply reflecting, the mirrors disclosed, divulged. Rather than a replicated, visual echo, they offered—out of the depths of the devotee's gaze—a form of response. We know the magic with which reflections, reflecting pools, and the first cast, hand-hammered mirrors were invested, in the founding mythologies of most

Mediterranean cultures. The reflection alone, properly interpreted, could disclose an otherwise invisible world of hidden realities. From *speculum*, the Latin word for mirror, we derive *speculation* and all that the word suggests in terms of wonder, mystery, the deep drift of the mind in its search for essential verities. Gregory of Nyssa believed that the mirror's reflection invited the individual to enter the very realm of the reciprocal. The soul, he claimed, partakes in beauty the instant it enters beauty's reflection. We might say the same for our votary. As her eye came to gaze on its own wobbling likeness, it might have encountered, in its hallucinatory fixation, that long-sought response. Out of the unfathomable depth of that depthless reflection, the divinity herself might have appeared, spoken, proffered her assistance.

We've always drawn sound from silence, coerced vision out of opacity. From reflective surfaces such as these Gallo-Roman votive mirrors, we've traditionally mined, extracted our realities. Once, though, instead of calling those realities "virtual," we considered them—as well we might—"veritable." Within these flickering disks, it's not merely the votary who saw herself reflected but—at any given instant—her beautiful counterpart, the goddess herself.

Dream Incubation ✐

THE TEMPLE AT RIEZ

Common throughout all antiquity, the practice of *incubatio*, or dream incubation, consisted of "sleeping in a temple or sacred place for oracular purposes."[1] Pilgrims would often travel considerable distances to reach such a temple or sanctuary in search of some divinely inspired dream vision. Within the sanctuary itself, they'd be placed in the care of officiating priests. These oneiromancers—versed in dream divination—would prepare the visitors' sleep by offering them the miraculous waters associated with the sanctuary, along with some soporific plant or medicinal concoction. Sleep, thereupon, would ensue. Responsible for maintaining the "dream hygiene" of their clients—keeping, that is, their bodies somnolent and their souls receptive so that the dreams might arrive undisturbed—the dream priests served as intermediaries between the human and the divine, between the realm of the conscious and that of the flickering screens of the subconscious itself.

Confined to a cubicle or *abaton* (a restricted dormitory), the visiting client, the "consulting party," would become the recipient of some dream, some codified message, sent by whichever divinity that particular sanctuary happened to honor. It might be said that the divinity, the sanctuary, and the miraculous waters associated with that sanctuary together formed a single oracular ensemble. Within that ensemble, the priest, practicing a form of sacerdotal medicine, would interpret the client's freshly received vision in terms of its curative or divinatory content. The dream itself was considered either remedial if the client happened to be ailing, or revelatory if the client happened to be in search of some visionary disclosure. In either case, the dream touched upon the immediate condition or state of mind of whoever came to consult the divinity in situ.

The practice of incubation (figuratively, the act of *covering* a dream like a still-incipient entity) has precedents that date from the dawn of recorded history. At first, dream visions weren't sought within the context of a sanctuary but, to the contrary, against the bare ground and beneath the vaulted dome of the night sky. Furthermore, they were induced autonomously: without the mediation, that is, of some attendant dream priest. We only have to think of Jacob lying in solitude against the desert floor, a stone for a pillow, dreaming the dream of the ladder. Greek literature abounds with references to similar "ear-to-ground" practices. Again and again, we have examples of vision-seekers lying naked against the bare earth or wrapped in the skin of some freshly sacrificed animal (often that of a black ram). This practice, we come to learn, was directly associated with Gaea, the earth goddess—the "mother of dreams," according to Euripides. We have abundant evidence in regard to an "archaic belief," as one prehistorian has put it, "touching on the relationship between earth herself (Gaea) and the rest of creation, for it's in the very bosom of the former that the mysterious seeds of life and the secrets of the future lie hidden."[2] Under propitious conditions, Gaea herself would reveal her most secret intentions. Lying against her earthen breast, the dreamer, having undergone the prescribed rites of purification, would receive—in some sudden, luminous, oneiric sequence—divine instruction.

It's difficult to determine when exactly those "seeds," those "hidden secrets" came to be considered the divine attributes of the heavens above as opposed to the earth below; when, in brief, Gaea and her circle of chthonic divinities found their powers usurped by a set of zealous, air-borne, male deities. Dreams, from that moment forth, would descend out of Olympian heights rather than rise out of the subsoils of a matricular earth. Zeus, in short, would supplant Gaea. Under his tutelage and that of his intermediaries—oneiropompists such as Hermes-Mercury—the very stuff of that subconscious world would undergo "virilization." Sanctuaries charged with the presence of a particular divinity would come to replace the earthen floor as appropriate for oracular reception. More than any other, the temple at Epidaurus in Greece, devoted to Asclepius, the god of medicine, became renowned for its receptive powers. Innumerable votive inscriptions, discovered in situ, attest to both the cures and revelations that transpired within its sacred chambers. Throughout the classical world, sanctuaries with their attendant priesthoods would come to practice incubation rites of their own. It is probable that such practices spread into Latinized Gaul, and that temples in the newly founded Provincia were constructed for expressly that purpose.

At Riez, for example, in Alpes-de-Haute-Provence, an inscription was discovered alongside the ruins of a Gallo-Roman temple that would lead us to believe that *incubatio* might well have been practiced on the site itself. What's more, within two hundred meters of the temple, an abundant spring gushes from the earth. Its waters have been considered miraculous since early antiquity, and continued to draw miracle-seekers (especially those afflicted with failing eyesight) until the beginning of the twentieth century. Waters such as these would be the first material attribute of any such sanctuary. Curative in their own right, they were a prerequisite for any form of iatromantic or medicodivinatory practice. Potions of those waters would be served to each visiting devotee before the latter entered into what has come to be called temple sleep.

The votive inscription at Riez reads to *Deo Aesculapio,* god of medicine and, as such, the Roman equivalent of Asclepius. Two observations come immediately to mind. First, like his Greek counterpart, Aesculapius was the son of Apollo. Aesculapius and Asclepius are inseparably related both by blood and by the curative powers with which they're each invested. Significantly enough, the name of Apollo, their father and the father of medicine, appears like a lost key in the full toponymic title to the city of Riez itself: *Colonia Julia Augusta Apolloinaris Reiorm.* The *Reiorm* would crystallize, finally, to "Riez." There is, then, a direct filial connection between these two therapeutic divinities, Apollo and Aesculapius, within the topological context of a relatively minor Gallo-Roman community. Furthermore, in a town nominally devoted to Apollo, an individual had left, as memento, a votive inscription to Apollo's son, Aesculapius. This rapprochement cannot be considered simply coincidental.

A second observation touches on the nature of the offerings themselves as stipulated in that carved limestone inscription. As tokens of gratitude, Aesculapius is designated the recipient of not merely two surgical instruments in silver and a gold torque, or "choker," decorated with snakes, but also a statuette in bronze of Somnus (*signum somni aereum*). All the mythopoeic elements associated with the practice of incubation, we discover, are herein reunited: a Gallo-Roman temple within immediate reach of a source reputed since antiquity as miraculous; an inscription dedicated to the god of medicine in a township named after his father, Apollo; and this little statuette of Somnus, the cherubic divinity of sleep.

Unfortunately, the bronze statuette has long since vanished. But we have a number of comparable works, depicting Somnus or his Greek counterpart, Hypnos, that date from the same period (the second century A.D.). Somnus is often portrayed in motion, striding forth, one foot placed before the other with wings sprouting from his temples. In one arm, he bears a bouquet of poppies; in the other, a *rhyton*, or drinking horn, filled presumably with miraculous waters. Youthful, light-footed, he always appears on the point of administering those soporific properties. Quite clearly the servant or accomplice of Aesculapius, he's as much the "anesthetist" as Aesculapius is the "practitioner." Together, they can be seen as the very deities, the dispensing agents, of incubation itself. It is they who bestow vision on the visitor; through the mediation of some officiating priest, they who restore health and spirits or disclose— through the esoteric medium of dreams—the future itself.

Indeed, what might surprise us today in studying oneiromancy in antiquity (as well as comparable practices in tribal societies throughout the world as revealed by modern ethnology) is the virtually exclusive emphasis their practitioners placed upon the future. Dreams, visions, induced hallucinations were all interpreted in terms of their eventual application in everyday life. As harbingers of the real, they anticipated reality, preceded event. One comes to realize that these antique societies were oriented—in their psychic disposition— toward their own evolution. They faced forward. Under rigorous sacerdotal supervision, the god-given visions that they experienced in temple sleep announced the forthcoming.

We, on the other hand, tend to face backward in our dream interpretations. Under the guidance of our own dream priests, we look to those "psychic vis-

*Fragment of a sculpture of Somnus, god of sleep.
A somniferous poppy hangs from his left hand; the snail
shell to the right signifies the magical properties of the
source with which the god is associated. Photo courtesy
Centre Camille Jullian, CNRS, Université de
Provence, Aix-en-Provence.*

itations" in the hope that they'll unlock otherwise inaccessible regions of
memory, give us glimpses of our all-too-obfuscated past. There, we know, still
lurk our angels and demons, the traumatic landscapes of our childhood, the
events—fictive or not—that have come to constitute our very being. We look
to those private dream worlds in the hope that, properly interpreted, they'll
allow us to come free of so many points of pure psychic fixation and enter, at
long last, the totality of the given instant: the present itself.

Here, though, we might come to sense something altogether different. Steeped as we are in history, be it personal or collective, charged (if not simply overwhelmed) by the accumulation of so much recorded event, we're apt to feel a certain fascination in contemplating the temple at Riez. For here, within immediate reach of its still gushing mineral springs, dreams were once read as fortunes, as signs of the imminent. Divine illuminations, they indicated the future for those relatively young Gallo-Roman societies. As for ourselves, wandering through these excavations two thousand years later, we can only speculate on such a vision. Late to the world, we can only feel a certain astonishment at the confidence these people must have enjoyed in a life which lay—with the mere closing of their eyelids—directly ahead of them.

Fervor and Residue 🐿

CHASTELARD-LARDIERS

We climb to that mountain sanctuary with little more, for equipment, than a pair of tweezers. For, once at the top, at the sanctuary itself, we begin spotting them: a quantity of minuscule bronze artifacts, far too small to pluck between our fingers. In rings, ringlets, perforated plaquettes rarely more than six or seven millimeters in diameter, they lie—acid green—against scattered patches of bare ground. At certain times of the year, especially after the last winter snows have vanished from the mountaintop, the ground virtually oozes bronze. Along with ceramic shards, these tiny artifacts come to crowd out even the pebbles themselves. Plucked like botanical specimens between the tongs of our tweezers, they tumble—one after another—into the well of some empty film canister.

We could become so engrossed collecting these devotional objects as to miss the sanctuary altogether. But it's the sanctuary itself that created the context, provided the milieu for such a rich vestigial accumulation. Founded in the first century A.D. on the grounds of a ruined, perhaps deliberately razed, Celto-Ligurian *oppidum*, itself dating from the fourth century B.C., Chastelard-Lardiers was once a pilgrimage site of immense importance. That pilgrims would travel astonishing distances to reach the sanctuary is attested by the provenance of the offerings they left. Seeking relief from some illness, the reversal of some misfortune, or, retroactively, "compensating" the local deity for some particular favor already granted, the pilgrims would arrive from as far north as the Seine basin and as far east as Lombardy. Making their way to the temple proper, they'd slip their bronze offerings (as well as rings, bracelets, an occasional gold laurel leaf from some victory garland) between the overlapping drystone walls along either side of the *via sacra* as they filed past.

Just beyond, at the temple itself, they would light tiny terra-cotta votive lamps. Over thirty thousand such lamps have been discovered in a *favissa*, a kind of disposal area similar to those that still exist for spent tapers in cathedrals. These terra-cotta votive offerings have provided archeologists with invaluable indications in regard to the rituals themselves. Small in comparison to traditional oil lamps (they are four to six centimeters in diameter) and devoid of any handle whatsoever, they were clearly intended to be laid in place on the altars themselves, rather than transported, carried about. They contained little oil and consequently wouldn't have burnt for more than about an hour. Those that burnt longer, quite clearly, were prohibited. This seemingly incidental observation gives us an idea, nonetheless, of the sheer numbers that must have crowded into the temple at certain moments. We may assume that the pilgrimage itself occurred at fixed times of the year in accordance with some cyclical votive celebration in honor of the local deity, Mars Belanos. Given the profusion at those particular moments, the pilgrims must have been hustled through the temple proper by the resident priests. What with the sheer press of so many devotees, they couldn't have been accorded more than a passing moment within. As to their votive lamps, scarcely lit, they'd have been swept away. For the altars, at such times, had to be kept continuously clear.

Descriptions of similar ceremonies, of the fervor of similar miracle-seeking crowds, exist throughout classical literature. Temples abounded with offerings. Some classicists such as Bötticher believe that the temples existed more for the sake of receiving and storing such offerings (even if, as here, the more ephemeral donations were immediately eliminated) than as places of sacred worship. The temples themselves were converted at such times into warehouses laden with the gifts of the fervent. The *cella*, or inner chamber, would lie virtually choked with an effusion of jewelry, boars' tusks, carved effigy. Lying on or before the altar itself, hanging from the surrounding colonnade or, alternatively, stacked one on top of the other, on so many crowded shelves, the offerings would proliferate. Often, too, they'd spill into the adjoining *pronaos*, or portico, before the temple proper; vases, bas-reliefs, trophies would even find themselves suspended from the temple's rooftop.

It's impossible to imagine today, on this empty, wind-swept plateau, such an accumulation of devotional artifacts. Impossible, for that matter, to imagine even the temple itself. Nearly nothing of that stout little structure remains but the barest outlines of a *cella* and its surrounding courtyard. Its white substructures rise no higher than the sallow grasses that languish at that altitude and the occasional outcrop, here and there, of stunted lavender. Even if we manage to pull our attention free of that underlying foundation long enough to admire the spectacular panorama that extends in every direction—the Alps to the east, the Sainte-Victoire to the south, and the Ventoux immediately to the west—we can't help but feel a certain desolation, a gathering *malaise*, in visiting this mountain sanctuary. For certainly we are standing, just here, at the base of a once fervently projected vertical: an invisible axis that ran, infallibly, between the throngs of the devout below and the divinity above. It matters little, in the last analysis, how the offerings, the ephemeral gifts of those guileless pilgrims, might have been received by the officiating priesthood, how they themselves might have been hustled through the sacred chambers on those prescribed days of pilgrimage. What matters, finally, is the axis itself, the vector it once provided between the secular and the sacred: the *address* it established between the world of the supplicant and that of the supplicated.

We pluck, gather, salvage whatever we can. The site itself, partially excavated by professional archeologists in the 1960s, has been ravaged in the past few years by *clandestins*: treasure seekers who have stopped at nothing in their search for gold bracelets, earrings, engraved seal rings—cultural merchandise far more "appreciable" than the tiny bits of worked bronze we manage to trap, occasionally, between the tongs of a common pair of tweezers. Dismantling entire walls, digging deep holes in the earth wherever their metal detectors have resounded positive, they've ignored these far less spectacular, far more significant/signifying materials altogether. Indeed, it's the relatively commonplace loops, ringlets, and plaquettes that we attempt to salvage ourselves. Far more, however, we attempt to classify all these relatively ephemeral offerings (the immense majority left, no doubt, by common folk) according to their respective typology. If, as we discover, the circle predominates, whether rolled in bronze wire or punctured into bronze plaquettes, the square, triangle, lozenge, and rectangle also occur with a certain regularity, suggesting a set of anatomical symbols. If the circle might well invoke, say, a wish for overall recovery, these more angular configurations could well have represented propitiatory wishes for specific organs or particular body functions. It's a hypothesis, at least, worth considering.

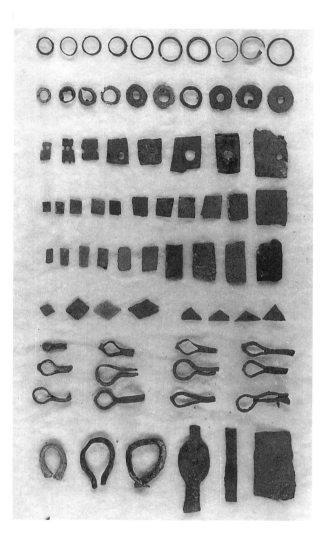

Bronze votive offerings from Chastelard-Lardiers:
rings, punctured plaquettes, squares, rectangles,
lozenges, triangles, "eyes," and amulets.
Photo by the author.

In studying any particular moment in history, one always arrives, it would seem, too late. Condemned to speculate, extrapolate, draw one's own tenuous arguments out of so much decontextualized material, one finds oneself at an ever-growing remove. The spiritually charged metaphors of one age have long since turned into the dull, devaluated metonyms of another. This is particularly true at Chastelard-Lardiers. Whether patiently gathered for a personal collection of votive archetypes, meticulously excavated by archeologists, or relentlessly looted by the *clandestins*, what is uncovered today constitutes little more than scrap metal, bent vestige, stray *bibelot*. All the incipient fervor with which these objects were once invested has vanished.

Hasn't that always been the case, however? We have sufficient material evidence to prove that these objects, as propitiatory vessels, never "outlasted" the vow or wish or expression of gratitude that they were charged to convey. We've seen, for instance, how the tiny terra-cotta lamps of those pilgrims, scarcely lit, were swept aside to make room for yet others. Snuffed, one might say, only moments after they'd been laid before the altar in supplication. By the tens of thousands, they were chucked into *favissae*, divested of all devotional properties whatsoever. Archeologists have even discovered large masses, scoriae, of smelted bronze within the very portico that surrounds the temple, suggesting that many of the metallic votive offerings might well have undergone similar "devaluations," been destroyed, like scrap metal, for the sake of recycling.

Given that the terra-cotta lamps and the bronze amulets served similar, if not identical, votive functions, we might speculate on the longevity of such functions. How long, for instance, could a prayer, a devotional supplication have lasted? Or, more exactly, how long could it have remained *active* and its material support, as such, inviolable? Being as urgent as it was ephemeral, the prayer would have lost its privileged status, as such, upon completion. Once addressed and, by implication, "received," it would have already fulfilled its function.

Now, nearly two thousand years later, we go about, tweezers in hand, picking at all this votive residue. Once, of course, each of these bronze artifacts, oozing up out of the mud, stood for a limb, an organ, a vital function, or, perhaps, some otherwise inadmissible wish. Once, indeed, for the span of a single, unrepeatable, vectorial instant, each of these spent tokens stood for an essential aspect of some individual's existence. Yes, one always arrives, it would seem, too late. Picking at a ringlet here, a lozenge there, so many acid green artifacts a bit everywhere, one is always laboring, it would seem, in the immense *post facto* of some existentially charged milieu. Drawn, now, out of all inherent context, the artifact—solidly pinched between the tongs of our tweezers, as if recuperated from so much millennial indifference—tumbles into the empty well of the film canister. Pure materialization of an immaterial volition, it has long since been divested of any transmissive value whatsoever. "Documentation" for the archeologists, pure "curio" for the rest, who can say that any object, in fact, outlasts the fires with which it was originally invested?

The place in itself doesn't exist before the bridge does.

HEIDEGGER, "BAUEN WOHNEN DENKEN,"
IN *VORTRÄGE UND AUFSÄTZE*

Le Pont Flavien

AN INSTANCE OF PASSAGE

With two identical triumphal arches at either extremity, the Pont Flavien—an elegant stone bridge dating from the Augustan Age—constitutes far more than a simple public conveyance. Located midway between Aix and Arles on the ancient Via Julia Augusta,[1] it appears—even from a distance—to stand in celebration of some long-forgotten event. But which, we might ask, as we approach the monument across a blighted, semi-industrialized landscape? What would have brought its donor, a certain Lucius Donnius Flavus (whence "Flavien"), to commission such a work in the first place, bequeathing, upon his death, sufficient funds for its construction?

Answers to these questions depend upon a closer examination of the bridge itself. Or, should we say, upon closer examination of the decor carved upon its twin arches. For the bridge, with a single barrel-vaulted archway and a clear span of no more than twelve meters, has little to distinguish it from other Roman bridges of the same period. Its identical triumphal arches, on the other hand, are quite distinctive. Built entirely out of bone white limestone, they rise

The Pont Flavien. Photo courtesy Harris Sobin.

on matching pilasters that seem to blossom, at their summit, into the rich floral arrangement of their stately Corinthian capitals. Just above these capitals rests the entablature. It's here, finally, at this level, in all the delicacy of the entablature's carved decor, that we come to recognize the singularity of the monument itself. At either end, an eagle, its wings half-spread and clutching in its claws the wreath of victory, faces inward onto the lacelike molding of the frieze as both its herald and its guardian. As herald, it serves to announce the "message" conveyed by the decorous frieze and the commemorative inscription that the frieze so richly envelops. As guardian, the eagle—protector of tombs in Latinized Gaul—keeps watch over the solemn decor it inaugurates.

With the Pont Flavien, we've entered, quite clearly, a heavily charged sym-

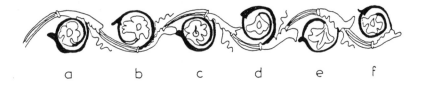

Drawing of a foliated scroll on the Pont Flavien.
Courtesy Anne Roth-Congès.

bolic milieu. Not only the eight inward-facing eagles but the foliated scroll of the molding and the inscribed cartouches that that molding encases all belong to a single consistent idiom: that of the funerary. We might say, in fact, that the bridge serves as nothing less than a cenotaph: an empty tomb, honoring the memory of its donor. The foliated scroll alone, a kind of unraveled funerary wreath, speaks eloquently of that memory, its perpetuation. An ongoing garland of pods, rosettes, and tendrils, it has been described best by Anne Roth-Congès in her definitive work on the bridge and on Augustan architecture in Provence generally: "Bursting forth between the leaves of a pod, a sheath in the form of a caulicle, itself slender and both fluted and enveloped by a collarette, gives birth—simultaneously—to a single-leafed bracteole, the stem of a floret and, between the two, an undulant, wire-thin tendril." She goes on to tell us that "tendrils and pods tend to repeat in exactly the same places and the flowers, either *Liliaceae* or *Iridaceae*, to resemble one another throughout."[2]

This floral decor might well be read as a graphically coded poem, designating, in the uninterrupted unraveling of its motif, the eternal, the self-perpetuating. As such, it might be seen, in semiotic terms, as the focal point—the very "message"—of the entire monument itself. More than the two virtually identical cartouches it envelopes on each of the facing arches, indicating the donor's name, the donation itself, and the names of those to whom its construction has been entrusted, this decor celebrates—in its florescent arabesques—a pictographic ode to the everlasting.

Finally, we come to the summit of the triumphal arches. There, we discover, stretched out on pediments at each of the arch's extremities, four limestone lions. Three of these lions, pure eighteenth-century bourgeois replicas, bear little or no resemblance to the fourth: a single surviving, thoroughly classic feline, dating from the construction of the bridge itself. If the three replicas assume somewhat slack, indolent, decorative poses, the fourth rears its hindquarters in wrath and clutches in a forepaw the severed head of its prey. We can't help but recognize in this figuration (despite the alarming degree of natural erosion it has undergone) the unmistakable function of the gorgon or gargoyle: an iconographic agent for warding off evil and protecting the edifice in all its symbolic integrity.

Throughout time, bridges have always been emblematic of passage. A space between spaces, the bridge has been seen as the point of mediation between the here and hereafter, earth and heaven, the human and the divine. Roth-Congès is quite explicit in regard to the Pont Flavien: "The arches," she writes, "sacrifice nothing to the triumphant in their primary role of representing passage."[3] Indeed, a good part of the hallucinatory charm of this particular edifice resides in its near perfect self-replication: its identical arches mirror each other so that passage in *either direction* becomes, symbolically speaking, an equally cathartic experience. Below, a little Provençal stream (the Touloubre) assumes, for the occasion, all the purifying attributes of the River Lethe, while above, the twin arches demarcate the limits of one life from that of the next. If passing underneath the first suggests death and departure, passing underneath the second can only promise—by the mediation of sign—arrival, admission, reception in a sacredly endowed "afterlife."

In a seminal essay entitled "Bauen Wohnen Denken" (Building dwelling thinking), Heidegger, meditating on the value of "place" in terms of human habitation, both in a spatial and ontological sense, chose "bridge" as a perfect exemplar of such habitation. In order that place be place, that thing be thing, it must summon unto itself, reassemble the fourfold: earth and air, the human and the divine. "Because," he writes, "only that which in itself is place (*Ort*) can accord place."[4] Only that which gathers under a single vocable, that is, the four constituent parts of presence itself can assure presence, establishing thereby our so-called being here. Heidegger continues:

> Whether its archways be raised or not, the bridge spans the river or ravine so that mortal man—whether he himself recognizes the transport of the bridge or not, he, who is forever en route toward some ultimate bridge—might strive to overcome his own sense of the habitual or the unworthy in order to approach, thereby, the integrity of the divine. The bridge *summons*, *reassembles*, because it serves as the impetus that allows passage unto the presence of the sacred. This holds true whether that presence is taken into consideration and ostensibly acknowledged, say, with an effigy on the bridge itself of its holy protector or that presence is totally ignored, even rejected, cast aside.
>
> The bridge, in its *own* manner, *gathers unto itself* earth and air, the mortal and the divine.[5]

One could hardly find a bridge more exemplary of the exemplar, more perfectly representative of the fourfold in all its constituent parts than the Pont Flavien. Here, in its reciprocal arches, "place," in uniting all the requisite elements for passage, establishes place. "Presence," in attesting to its own translation, assures presence. A "here," in vouchsafing for a reciprocal "there," gives full, iconographic expression to an instance of sheer unequivocal being.

In commissioning this work two thousand years ago to commemorate his own passage, Lucius Donnius Flavus left in legacy a monument by which others might recognize the emblems of their own passage, their own deliverance. Today, we cannot help but recognize, in the interreflective mirrors of these two wind-worn arches and the little stone bridge that they bracket, the symbolic decor that might prompt us to reevaluate our own sense of the "transmissive," the "transcendent." Here, in the given image, we might recognize the given reflection; in the "one," acknowledge the "other." And, so doing, in this perfect set of reciprocities, undergo a certain sense of passage ourselves.

in memory of René Char

PART IV

Aquaeductus ⤳

There is no source that is not sacred.

SENECA, *EPISTLES*

The ruins of aqueducts and sepulchers lay about everywhere: ruins that
seemed more like the forests and indigenous plants of an earth composed
of the dust of the dead and the debris of empires.

CHATEAUBRIAND, *VOYAGE EN ITALIE*

Aquaeductus 🖎

I

Running in a sequence of dismembered sections, the Roman aqueduct of Nîmes
can be read as a kind of fragmented antique text. Its choked tunnels, collapsed
archways, brief truncated arcades can be seen as the scattered passages, say, of
some early ontological discourse. This discourse (*dis-* + *currere*: to run forth
or asunder) expressed itself, no doubt, in terms of the fluent, the continuous.
Even today, there's not an isolated pier, a hydraulic cross section that doesn't
draw one's attention as some severed part of a dynamic ensemble: a hiatus at
the running heart of a once unbroken continuum.

From the source onward, one can interpret the full length of this "linear
edifice"[1] as a sequence of scattered phrases, parenthetical clauses, even—at
the very limit—sprays of infinitesimal punctuation. For the entire structure
begs to be read. Out of so many disarticulated units, it seems to await nothing
less than its own restitution through the agency of some synthesizing grammar. The least element matters. Isolated plinths, conduits, panels of rose red

A section of the Roman aqueduct of Nîmes.
Photo by the author.

aggregate: there's nothing that wouldn't serve that restitution. Not a pebble that wouldn't enter, finally, that inherent discourse.

Curiously enough, one hears the source before actually seeing it. It bubbles, quite audibly, from underneath the weeds of an abandoned orchard before gushing forth—fifteen, twenty meters later—as a limpid little brook. Why had the Romans chosen this particular site, these waters? The Fontaine d'Eure, located just beneath the perched medieval city of Uzès, satisfies the two basic conditions for determining an aqueduct's point of inception. The first, of course, touches upon the quality of the water itself. It needed to be as pure, as salutary as possible. Vitruvius suggests in his masterly *De architectura* that one can determine the quality of water emanating from a particular source by the health of those who happen to live in its immediate vicinity. "If they are hardy, of fine complexion, subject to neither inflammations of the eye nor pains in the leg, then one can be assured of the water's goodness." Vitruvius also recommends sprinkling a few drops onto the finest copper plate available. If the drops leave no stain, then the water, he claims, may be considered perfectly pure.[2]

The second basic condition that the Fontaine d'Eure satisfies is that of altitude. It is located at a point sufficiently elevated to allow the water in its catchment basin to flow the full fifty-one-kilometer length of the aqueduct—from, that is, the plateau of Uzès to the plains of Nîmes—powered by nothing more than the force of gravity. In terms of hydraulic engineering, the achievement was monumental. Not only did the waters of the Fontaine d'Eure traverse that expanse, they forded a major river (the Gardon), crossed at least eleven substantial highland valleys, and tunneled through several hundred meters of solid limestone before reaching—an estimated twenty-six hours and forty-five minutes later—the *castellum*, or underground water reservoir, of Nîmes itself. All the while it maintained a gradient that averages, throughout, no more than twenty-four centimeters a kilometer, or, approximately, an inch every few hundred feet. Given the sheer immensity of the structure, this gradient can only be seen as something infinitesimal. Mass, here, was brought to serve virtually imperceptible increments of measure.

So, from the outset, the source, both for its altitude and the purity of its waters, must have attracted the *libratores*, those Roman land surveyors responsible for locating such waters and laying out the trajectory for an aqueduct's passage. But for us, standing at the exact same point today, the aqueduct's debut isn't altogether that evident. At its inception, all we can see, running along the shadow-dappled edge of a public playground, are the first truncated sections of a derelict conduit. The first, interrupted phrases of that projected discourse. Call them, if you will, its initial stutters.

An aqueduct, however, no matter how dilapidated, draws the visitor with a distinct magnetism of its own. Unlike the oval outline, say, of an antique arena or the embedded *D* of an excavated amphitheater, an aqueduct, eminently sequential by nature, tugs at the senses, invites one to follow—in so many broken segments—its singular route across gullies and ridgelines, through orchards and scrub oak. Discourse, indeed. For we feel immediately involved, implicated in the running of this historic program. It suggests, no doubt, *other* conduits, *other* passageways: those that function at subjective levels unto themselves. So doing, an aqueduct offers us a set of analogous images for our own personal sense of rupture, fragmentation, discontinuity. Reading its vestiges, we cannot help but feel that we're interpreting something of ourselves. That we're attempting to reconstitute, no matter how subliminally, sections of our own obliterated itinerary, that *its* text might very well underlie *our own*.

II

The Romans considered fresh running water as something precious, even sacred. *Mirabilia aquarum*, they repeatedly called it: wonderous waters. Rome alone, at its peak, was serviced by no less than nine aqueducts, and the city itself languished in the spray of an estimated 1,352 public fountains. Night and day, water would "overflow its basins, filling the city's pools, brimming over the edges of both the dyer's and the fuller's vat, gushing up in the midst of gardens, pouring over into public baths and spacious *thermae*, then, purging la-

trines, end finally in those very gutters wherein everything, once, first originated."[3] Indeed, to appreciate the extent to which Rome invested its waters with
near magical properties, one might, in passing, recall those origins. For Rome,
at the beginning, was little more than a cluster of seven hills sitting in the midst
of a fluvial marshland. Romulus and Remus were rescued as little babies from
that very marshland, thanks to the intervention of the she-wolf. Much of
Rome's early history, as well as its founding mythology, was based, in fact, on
the manner in which it came to drain those marshes and, at the same time, harness the distant spring waters of the Apennines to serve its growing needs. It
might even be said that Rome (and, by extension, the entire Roman Empire)
evolved out of a deep-seated dialectic between the still and the flowing, the
stagnant and the animate: between an ever-inherent, regressive tendency toward death (the "death wish") and, far more manifest, toward life. To channel, sluice, furnish entire populations with fresh water must have represented,
for the *mens romana*, an all-powerful affirmation of existence itself. It was a
means by which Rome could express domination over its own paludal origins.
Could surmount, like some lower level of consciousness, its own groundless
past: that "Rome of Romulus," as Cicero described it, "steeped in mud."[4]

As perhaps its proudest achievement, the construction of aqueducts, whether
for the mother city itself or any of its innumerable outlying colonies, followed
the same rigorous set of operational procedures. First, as already mentioned,
came the *libratores*. From *libramentum*, a noun signifying the action by which
a particular surface may be determined level, the *libratores* employed no more
than two basic instruments: the *groma*, an ungainly, stiltlike platform from
which dangled four lead-weighted plumb lines, assuring, once adjusted, astonishingly accurate horizontal sight-of-eye readings, and the *chorobate*, a
wooden table no less than six meters long upon which lay a traditional sur-

veyor's level: a glass tube with its ever-vagabond water bubble. The *chorobate* was particularly useful on windy days when the strict verticality of the *groma's* plumb lines could no longer be assured.

For us, making our way over the broken terrain of the Languedocian moors, rife with gullies, abrupt ledges, and sudden patches of impenetrable undergrowth, it's virtually impossible to imagine how those *libratores* came to take such infinitesimally fine measurements. Not only did they manage to establish a gradient far too slight for our own senses to appreciate, they projected over that broken ground, in so many loops, zigzags, and hill-hugging contours, a single, seamless trajectory. Nothing mattered in all their calculations but the proper flow of the waters themselves. For the flow needed to be maintained at a speed slow enough to keep the waters from eroding the U-shaped channel of the conduit itself (the *specus*), yet fast enough to reach—in a single, uninterrupted run—the *castellum* of Nîmes without losing their essential freshness.

Ours, we'd claim, coming upon the barrel-vaulted entry, say, of some underground hydraulic section or a stranded pier, standing in the midst of a cherry orchard. Yes, *ours*, we'd repeat, taking an instinctive, proprietorial interest in something we can only claim by analogy, by the running metaphor of its disparate parts. These parts, however, suffice. Lying like clues to our own sense of a lost underlying unity, they become the objects—the cherished objects— of an intense scrutiny. Measured, correlated, treated as the semantically charged particles of that otherwise obliterated discourse, the least vestige receives extravagant attention.

A large part of the Nîmes aqueduct (of most aqueducts, for that matter) was constructed underground. Its buried sections account for over sixty percent of its total trajectory. This was the *rivus subterraneus*, celebrated by Frontinus. Yet another twenty percent runs flush against the surface of the ground

An underground section of the aqueduct.
Photo by the author.

(be it soil or bedrock), the conduit itself capped by a succession of heavy, over-hanging stone slabs. These figures, however, shouldn't surprise us. For doesn't our own hidden discourse—that elusive script—travel sub rosa from its very inception, concealing, as it goes, far more than it reveals? Suggesting in a sub-liminal grammar of its own, so much more than it chooses to disclose.

Less than twenty percent, or nine kilometers, of the total structure conforms to one's traditional vision of a Roman aqueduct. Running overhead on either a solid masonry support (*opus caementicium*) or, whenever its total height exceeded six meters, on a series of vaulted arches (*opus arcuatum*), the elevated sections of the aqueduct astonish us with their inherent unity. Even if most of those sections have undergone irreparable depredation and we find ourselves staring, for the most part, at truncated vestiges, we're struck, nonetheless, by an uninterrupted sense of the serial—the rhythmically determined—running throughout. There's not a single stranded archway that doesn't exude—out of every pore of its still adherent, still articulated masonry—something of the pulsate. Caryatids, we might call them. In an unbroken processional, these water bearers had once cradled that precious element as it traveled at a rate of no less than a one hundred cubic meters a minute against the very crooks of their mineral necks.

We're involved, here, with movement. Despite the apparent petrification of so many isolated elements, we're witnesses to an initial dynamic: that drafted by the architects themselves. For no sooner had the *libratores*, those expert land surveyors, completed their work (laying out the aqueduct's trajectory and clearing, at the same time, a swath of ground thirty meters wide for its construction) than the responsibility for the entire project devolved upon the *architecti*. Their role, according to antique sources, was exclusively conceptual. They were charged, first and foremost, with maintaining *proportio*: a word we might translate as "harmony." It's this very harmony, this underlying sense of architectonic unity, that we continue to recognize in visiting the aqueduct's surviving sections. Masters of number, scale, and proportion, the *architecti* were charged with creating—out of an endless succession of telluric accidents—the vector of a single, singular, uninterrupted, water-bearing conduit.

The final responsibility for the construction itself, however, fell upon its *redemptores* or building contractors. It was they who chose the materials for the entire edifice and oversaw its execution from beginning to end. We are fairly certain that these *redemptores,* or *locatur operis,* were native to the very region in which they operated. They needed to be perfectly familiar with whatever resources happened to be immediately at hand, most especially in regard to quarries: to the quality and characteristics of the stone in each, and to the competence of the quarriers from one site to the next. Furthermore, they needed to provide immediate answers to an endless series of logistical problems touching upon the acquisition, transportation, and final deployment of every conceivable material, from crushed amphorae for the cement aggregates to monolithic keystones weighing, quite often, several tons each. Their familiarity with the region needed to be total.

It's almost impossible to imagine the sheer magnitude of the worksites these *redemptores* were called upon to oversee. We know that tens of thousands of laborers—mostly slaves—executed the bulk of the work under the immediate command of the military. Then, too, innumerable artisans, specialists in their own particular fields, assured the execution of the finer, more applied aspects of the overall construction. Along with the presence of so many teeming quarriers, stone carvers, and masons, there were the carpenters, assembling, in situ, the indispensable trusses, scaffolds, and hoists for the overhead sections; the blacksmiths, honing tools and pounding out heavy iron holdfasts to an-

chor one monolithic voussoir against another; the itinerant lime burners sup-
plying the stonemasons with an unending quantity of fresh mortar as they
traveled—at the same relentless yet imperceptible speed—down the full length
of that gargantuan worksite. To all the above must be added the carters, the
cartwrights, the entire armies employed in the transportation of everything
from firewood for feeding the lime kilns to the meats and fruit and wine jugs
for nourishing that immense population in its immeasurably slow migration
downward.

In reviewing the multiple aspects of the overall project, we mustn't lose sight
of the one structural element that ultimately mattered: the *specus*, or conduit.
For there wasn't a bucket of mortar or a spadeful of gravel that didn't serve,
finally, as support for that sleek, lime-faced, U-shaped conveyor. Measuring
no more than 1.30 meters in width and 1.80 meters in height throughout its full
fifty-one-kilometer throw, the conduit was the *raison d'être*, after all, for the
entire structure. No matter how deep the aqueduct's tunnels or colossal its
vaulted overhead arcades, nothing mattered, in the end, but that narrow, meticulously prepared corridor in which the water, precious as it was salutary, would
run in a single unbroken current. When the *specus* wasn't carved directly in
rock, its bedding consisted of poured cement plaster, its parallel uprights of
joined stone masonry, and its overhead vaulting of massive tabletop limestone
slabs. Throughout its entire trajectory, in fact, water would run sheltered beneath one kind of covering or another. Thus protected from the intrusions of
man and animal alike as well as the injurious effects of sunlight (*"ut minime
sol aquam tangat,"* specifies Vitruvius: the less sunlight touching the water, the
better),[5] it would arrive perfectly fresh at its destination. Infallibly, that destination would be the city itself. As one archeologist has phrased it, if an aqueduct was essentially rural in its trajectory, it remained ultimately urban in its

ambition.[6] For the Romans, with their vision fixated upon the city—the *idea* of city as the concentrate of every civilized value—the aqueduct could only be at the service of *urbanitas*.

It should be noted, in passing, that the *specus* or corridor in which the waters traveled lay lined with several coats of waterproofing mortar. Called *opus signinum*, this mortar consisted of a lime in which a rich aggregate of broken tile, brick, and crushed amphorae had been added. Applied in two, sometimes three layers, the mortar was then sealed by a thin, lacquerlike wash of scarlet-colored pigment. According to Pliny the Elder, this ultimate layer of waterproofing was composed of nothing less than quicklime, slaked in wine, and mollified, in turn, with an admixture of fig juice and pork fat. The result, he claimed, was the most tenacious substance on earth (*"res omnium tenacissima"*) and would outlast even stone in sheer durability.[7]

It's up to us to imagine these waters flowing at such speed, with such abundance, reflecting in their passage the unctuous reds of their immediate surroundings. To imagine the unimpaired flow of thousands of cubic meters per hour traveling—tobogganlike—down a whole series of sinuous curves only to enter, immediately after, a nearly flat, nearly imperceptible gradient for the sake of reaching—a full day later—the deep recipient basins of Nîmes. Up to us, finally, to imagine such a seamless construction; reconstitute, out of all its sparse, surviving segments, such a resolute view of the indivisible.

III

There are two ways, essentially, to read an aqueduct: ideally, as a resuscitated ensemble, or pragmatically, as a suite of dismembered sections. We've chosen the latter. Beginning with the little that remains, we've gone from one isolated archway to another, one stout little culvert (smothered, nowadays, in ilex, juniper, in the iridescent pink sprays of the terebinth) to the next. Haunted, no doubt, by *other* conduits, *other* conveyors, we've created an analogy of our own. Out of an innate sense of some fundamental continuum, running in the deepest channels of our consciousness, we've come to interpret vestige, here, as script. Begun reading its fragments as our own.

Curiously enough, this analogy, this extended metaphor, seems to lose its effectiveness in the face of the aqueduct's one major surviving monument, the Pont du Gard. For the bridge itself is far too well preserved to invoke one of those lost, mnemonic passages. It might even be said that the Pont du Gard suffers, in this context, from a certain *absence of absence*. Rising a full forty-eight meters over the green, pellucid Gardon on three successive tiers of vaulted masonry, this "masterpiece of functional architecture" suggests nothing more than itself.[8] Rousseau, in visiting the bridge in the 1730s, would exult: "The overall appearance of this noble if austere work impresses me all the more for standing in the midst of a wilderness where the surrounding silence and solitude render the monument that much more striking and one's admiration that much more entire, given that this so-called bridge is but a simple aqueduct."[9]

As for ourselves, however, we need to explore that "surrounding silence and solitude," need to rummage through the heavy undergrowth of these Languedocian moors for the sake of that fracture, that fragment, that stray archeological signifier lying in the midst of our long vanished discourse. It's as if only the shattered, the disjuncted, had "something to say." As if only the estranged could speak, finally, in the name of that all too elusive integer.

So here we are, having crossed the Pont du Gard (crouching as we went within the low corridor of its overhead *specus*) and entered, immediately after, the Bois de Remoulins. From this point onward, the aqueduct breaks once again into disconnected sections. Moving, now, through a wilderness of low, wind-stunted dwarf oak, we feel a sudden rush of pleasure whenever we happen upon a few meters of masoned conduit in one place, the rounded right angle of an elbow bend in yet another. For, in so doing, we've identified a portion of that decimated itinerary. Encountered, once again, a piece of our own obscure puzzle. Recognized, in a brief corridor of bedrock, part of that running, self-proclaimed metaphor. For it's not an aqueduct, finally, that we're tracking, but ourselves. Not the disparate sections of some historical monument, but the diaphanous outlines of some long since obliterated human program.

Monument and metaphor: the history of one illustrates the ideation of the other. Through an examination of the former, we might come to a greater understanding of the latter; taking measure of so much given, material evidence, come to appreciate all the more the drifting vocables of our own drawn analogy, that "parallelogram" of sorts we've created for ourselves.

We should begin, then, by distinguishing three distinct periods in the history of the aqueduct: that of its construction (essentially under the reign of Claudius in the middle of the first century A.D.); that of its maximal flow and distribution (a period covering the subsequent three centuries); then that, by far the longest and easily the most evocative, of its dismantlement and ultimate destruction. If we linger here on the last of these three periods, it's only to appreciate more fully the analogies we might draw in terms of our own personal sense of the disaggregated. For comparisons clearly abound. The breakdown of such a monolithic public service, functioning for the general benefit, had already begun. We find, for example, the first cases of illicit water-tapping (the clandestine diversion of that public commodity for the sake of satisfying private, essentially agrarian needs) already manifest by the end of the fourth century. These first instances of pirated waters can be attributed to local landowners deliberately creating breaches in the aqueduct or simply canalizing its spillage for the sake of irrigating their crops in immediately adjacent areas. Piles of porous, tufaceous concretions, laying flush against the walls of the aqueduct, still attest to this practice. These piles, standing like frozen cascades, became more and more frequent as the fifth century progressed and indicate a profound change in the operational life of the aqueduct. Colonists (essentially retired centurions, massively compensated) began replacing, at this time, small autochthonous landowners. These new settlers would tap and thus reduce the flow of the aqueduct in ever-increasing quantities. We can only assume that they did so with the tacit approval, if not the active complicity, of whatever authorities happened to be responsible for the water's distribution.

We have then, and increasingly, the first indisputable evidence of a breakdown in the functioning of the aqueduct as originally conceived: as a uniform construct at the service of a singular entity, the *res publica*. More and more, the vested interests of a new landed gentry would determine the flow and distribution of that public commodity; the aqueduct would come to serve the few at the expense of the many. "Great country villas and the large domains that sprang up around them with their constituent settlers (*coloni*) would lead to the total breakdown of the Roman aqueduct. From this new set of conditions," writes Albert Grenier, "a closed economy would emerge, replacing the rich exchanges that once existed in which cities served as metropolises."[10]

Archeologists, studying both the quantity and quality of these waters, their "paleoflow" as evinced by tiny laminal, concretionary deposits found along the inner walls of the *specus* itself, have detected traces of increasing turbidness throughout the fifth century. Concretionary deposits have given them a remarkable basis for interpreting the *life* of the aqueduct, especially in its years of degenerescence. They've learned, for example, that the fresh running waters that traveled down its conduit through the second, third, and fourth centuries left a clear, near-crystalline deposit called "travertine," but that those same waters a century later, obstructed by organic matter, tended to grow muddy and turbid, generating, as concretion, a rough, porous substance called tufa.

Clearly, the aqueduct no longer received the kind of continuous care that it had in the past. *Circitores*, maintenance workers charged with its upkeep, no longer journeyed up and down its length, scrubbing the walls clean and keeping vegetation from invading its low, lidded, ongoing chamber. Roots now dangled from the vaulted slabs overhead. Reaching into the canal itself, these roots not only inhibited the flow of the water and raised, consequently, its level, but also introduced the algae and bacteria that would decompose and form the aforementioned concretions. This process, called biolithogenesis, is caused by the interaction of karstic waters (heavily charged with lime or calciferous matter) and organic substances which were introduced by the root systems.

Increasingly choked by its own concretions, the aqueduct would supply less and less water to the *civitas* of Nîmes. By the end of the fifth century, its yield had fallen from an optimal 124,000 cubic meters per day to an estimated 14,630. At the same time, the quality of this water had gone from limpid and crystalline to something turbid, unpotable, and fit for little more than purging the city's underground sewerage system. We may assume from these figures that the aqueduct must have suffered increasingly from the absence of a single centralized agency responsible for its upkeep. In fact, everything indicates a breakdown, an atomization of any such authority. The unity of this eminently transmissive structure could no longer be assured.

We may also assume that the last to benefit from its waters weren't the citizens of Nîmes, but those prosperous landowners, latifundians and the like, on their flourishing plantations. Turbid or not, the waters would continue to irrigate their orchards and vineyards, and the landowners would continue to benefit individually from what had once been an exclusively public commodity. Metaphor, indeed. For how can we help but see—as if mirrored within this particular, historic complex—an image of our own collective breakdown? How can we help but discover, in these remote landscapes, a paradigm for our own structural fragmentation; in its diverted waters, elements of that very same truncated discourse?

Worse, far worse, awaited the aqueduct. Having undergone *de facto* privatization and fallen into the hands of disparate interests, it was reduced from a rushing cataract to a mere trickle of turbid water. Even that trickle, however, would undergo sporadic arrests as, for instance, during the Great Invasions when Nîmes was repeatedly besieged. By the sixth century, even that trickle, that meager yield, would have ceased. Obliged to erect or reinforce their defense systems against the invading Franks and Visigoths, local populations fell upon the aqueduct itself as a storehouse of readily available materials. Out of its hydraulic masonry arose ramparts, watchtowers, strongholds. No doubt the invading armies, both Franks and Visigoths, did much the same themselves. Warring simultaneously against one another and the local Gallo-Roman populations, they ransacked whatever they could. Within a brief period of time, then, this singular construction, now only the ghost of that once gushing conduit, was converted into a public stone quarry. One could pillage at will. With its massive blocks pried loose, disassembled and carted off, the overall structure came to resemble some slain mastodon, its flanks hacked into so many hopelessly divided sections.

Throughout the Middle Ages, the aqueduct would continue to suffer the abuse (or simple indifference) of historic circumstances. Alain Malissard, in

Les Romains et l'eau, has drawn a moving portrait of those dark times. Everywhere in the ex-Roman Empire, he tells us, aqueducts suffered the same fate.

> The underground canals would slowly collapse under the weight of rubble and ruin; vestiges of an impossible level of well-being, hopelessly incrusted now, choked in silt, cracked, perforated, dismantled by anyone who happened to be in search of building materials, the overhead sections of the aqueduct would tumble, one after another, into a countryside gone thoroughly fallow.[11]

This demolition wouldn't reach its peak, however, until the Romanesque, five centuries later. Then, in what often has been called "the first renaissance," a whole *corpus* of monks, lay-brothers, and ecclesiastics of all rank, serving as masons, stone carvers, and architects, would set upon and pillage the aqueduct in an unprecedented manner. There was, indeed, an out-and-out ravaging of the edifice during the period between 1050 and 1200. In deciding which particular sector to reclaim, three critical factors determined the choice for that be-frocked work force: first, that the sector be part of some overhead section (the stones there being more accessible, easier to dislodge); second, that the sector be as near as possible to the worksite itself, whether chapel, church, or monastery; and third, that no other source of building material (a contemporary stone quarry, for example) be within immediate reach. For that reason, some of the finest surviving segments of the aqueduct run directly through areas that are still rich in quarries. As for the rest, however—the greater part of the aqueduct, that is—the Romanesque would make short work of that massive structure. Pried loose, disassembled, its stones would reappear now out of all established context. Sprouting in the form of plinths, capitals, altar pieces, they'd have undergone total dislocation. Far more than the quarried stones themselves, however, the concretions lying flush against the *specus*—that once waterproofed conduit—would constitute the most prized building material of all.

Easy to carve and offering a single perfectly uniform surface, these travertine incrustations could be dressed into highly decorative blocks resembling—in both granulation and luster—marble itself. Scarcely more than fossilized water, than the petrification of that water within so many successive laminal plates, these slabs would make their way into a jamb here, a lintel there, a particular architrave there again. Today, following the last remaining traces of the aqueduct itself, one is likely to find, within a swath of land no more than two or three kilometers on either side, blocks of that lovely concretion rippling like candy stripes in the midst of so much commonplace masonry. Not only chapels, churches, and monasteries became the beneficiaries of this legitimized plunder, but castles, keeps, outlying domains, even—on occasion—dovecotes, barns, the least agricultural dependency. Everywhere individual interests, secular or sacred, came to feed on that long, winding, vectorial ruin. The *res publica*, that prescription in favor of the all, ended in this free-for-all pillaging by the each.

The aqueduct's dismantlement continued well past the Romanesque. Each succeeding period in history would bring its own distinctive contribution to its unmaking. One might even postulate a typology, an entire methodology, devoted exclusively to the *praxis* of its demolition. During the seventeenth and eighteenth centuries, for instance, peasants reclaiming fallow land in the surrounding hillsides needed a considerable quantity of stone for creating *restanques*, terraced retaining walls against soil erosion. The stones for these bulwarks came, often enough, from that long-since desiccated watercourse. The aqueduct's once seamless structure was little more, now, than a narrow, ongoing strip of disposable rubble.

It was the construction, however, of an irrigation canal, the Canal de Pouzin, in the 1860s that would strike a last, definitive blow to the edifice, most especially in the final fifteen-kilometer leg of its trajectory. Here, the hydraulic engineers of the past century could think of nothing better than laying their own canal directly over that of the Roman: pouring, that is, their own industrial cement over the antique *opus signinum*, not only cloning the aqueduct, but smothering it irreparably in a glut of protomodern agglomerates.

The aqueduct today, as it approaches what was once its final destination, the *castellum* of Nîmes, seems to vanish altogether. It's as if our text, our imaginary discourse, at the very moment when it might have reached some kind of conclusion, underwent a form of deletion. Suffered a kind of censorship. Granted, one can still come across the brief parenthetical clause of some barrel-vaulted conduit, or the paraphrase of some sinuous, subterranean diversification. Any hope, however, of bringing the sporadic fragments of that tenuous discourse to closure has long since vanished. In its final kilometers, the aqueduct finds itself consumed by a succession of suburbs, commercial centers, industrial parks. We're no longer drawn, guided, by visible evidence, by a rhythmic set of vaulted arcades or a single Piranesian archway standing in the midst of some rocky, Cezannesque landscape. There's not even a three-meter swath of stunted wheat running clear across a field of grain to indicate the unmistakable presence, just beneath, of that indomitable edifice. Caught now in the labyrinthine underworld of a fully serviced modern city, the aqueduct dies an obscure death. Running beneath the streets, gardens, workshops of an increasingly congested metropolis, it finds itself hopelessly broken into brief, isolated units. Some of those units have been converted into individual cisterns, cesspools, latrines, serving their particular proprietor immediately overhead. Yet others have seen their vaulted chambers turned into private storage spaces, woodsheds, even wine cellars. Of that gargantuan, fifty-one-kilometer thrust of pure human inspiration, motivated by nothing less than a single overriding public necessity, little if anything remains within the cellulated underworld—the larders, crypts, choked passageways—of contemporary Nîmes.

Quite recently, yet another form of depredation has come to undermine the aqueduct. This time, however, it's not the structure per se that finds itself endangered, but the very idea underlying its existence. Several archeologists have come to question the motivations that led to such an extravagant construction in the first place. Was it, in fact, really necessary, they've asked? Didn't Gallo-Roman Nîmes in the time of Claudius already possess a sufficient water supply, thanks to both an abundance of natural springs and a rich network of cisterns for recuperating rainwater? Wasn't the elaboration of such a colossal project merely an act of manifest bravura, undertaken more for the sake of prestige—sheer ostentation—than for the service it actually rendered in the form of all that pure, gushing, unarrested water?

We, of course, can only reject such an argument. We've grown far too attached to the aqueduct, to its *necessity* as both monument and metaphor, both structure and sign, to endorse such a slender hypothesis that figures alone—the simplest calculations—could readily refute. Furthermore, these ruins, we feel, have long since become an indispensable part of our culture. Even hopelessly dilapidated, they still manage to signify a sense, indicate a direction, offer (no matter how segmented) a magnanimous image of the sequential in its full functional capacity as distributing agent. It's not for nothing that we've attempted to read, and reading, interpolate those gagged channels and collapsed archways in terms of a truncated antique text. Not for nothing that we've come to recognize—no matter how diaphanously—whole portions of that limpid, life-sustaining discourse as if inscribed within its still-surviving sections. Ruins like this, after all, are what we've inherited. What, ultimately, we possess. Their lost grammar—almost certainly verdant, pellucid—is what we've been given, in turn, to interpret, transcribe, perpetuate.

Notes 〰

TERRA AMATA

1. Musée de Terra Amata, 25 boulevard Carnot, 06300 Nice.

THE FIRST HUNTERS AND THE LAST

1. André Dumoulin, personal conversation with the author, 1979.

2. Marshall Sahlins, *Stone Age Economics* (Chicago: Aldine-Atherton, 1972).

NEOLITHICIZING PROVENCE

1. Recent carbon-14 analyses of the Cardial at L'Abri de la Font-des-Pigeons situate its earliest, ceramic vestiges somewhere between 4600 and 3600 B.C.

2. Jean Courtin, "Le Néolithique ancien de la Provence," in *Colloque sur l'épi-paléolithique méditerranéen* (Paris, Editions du CNRS, 1975), 198.

3. V. Gordon Childe, *The Dawn of European Civilization*, 6th ed. (New York: Knopf, 1958).

4. Gabriel Camps, "La Provence préhistorique," in *La Provence des origines à*

l'an mil: Histoire et archéologie, ed. Paul-Albert Février et al. (Paris: Editions Ouest-France, 1989), 130–131.

ARCHEOLOGICAL RHETORIC

1. Hector Nicolas, *Une excursion à Bonnieux et à Buoux*: *Mémoires de l'Académie de Vaucluse* (Avignon: Académie de Vaucluse, 1886), 214–223.

2. Didier Binder, *Le Néolithique ancien provençal: Typologie et technologie des outillages lithiques* (Paris: Editions du CNRS, 1987), 15, 34, 35.

MOON GODDESS

1. Mircea Eliade, *Traité d'histoire des religions* (Paris: Editions Payot, 1949), 116–117. Therein Eliade declares: "The Moon operates on a level of human consciousness that not even the most corrosive form of rationality can possibly reach." (My translation.)

THE SKULL WITH THE SEASHELL EAR

The archeological materials for this essay have been drawn from Odile Roudil and Georges Bérard, *Les sépultures mégalithiques du Var* (Paris: Editions du CNRS, 1981), 102–106.

1. Rainer Maria Rilke, *Letters to a Young Poet*, trans. Reginald Snell (London: Sidgwick and Jackson, 1945), 21.

WEST-SOUTHWEST

1. Gérard Sauzade, *Les sépultures du Vaucluse du Néolithique à l'Age du Bronze* (Marseilles: Editions du Laboratoire de paléontologie humaine et de préhistoire; Paris: Institut de paléontologie humaine, 1983), 283. Translation mine.

2. See Roudil and Bérard, *Les sépultures mégalithiques du Var.*

3. Claude Masset, *Les dolmens: Sociétés néolithiques, pratiques funéraires* (Paris: Editions Errance, 1993), 15.

4. Ibid., 87.

5. Notions of so-called human progress are quickly dispelled in reading osteological reports on excavated bone deposits. Analyses often show a far healthier, more advanced state of development of bone tissue in the Neolithic than, say, the Medieval, three to four thousand years later.

6. Roudil and Bérard, *Les sépultures mégalithiques du Var*, 173.

7. Eliade, *Traité d'histoire des religions*, 124 ff.

8. It would be interesting to pursue, from a prehistorian's perspective, Eliade's fascinating exposé on "Uranian divinities." In moving from the passive to the active, from the archaic "lunar-chthonic-agrarian divinities" (unmistakably female) to the "fecundating-atmospheric" figures of the sun gods, haven't we, in mythological terms, a perfect reflection of the immense material transformations that humanity underwent upon entering the Neolithic and, most especially, the "harnessing of nature" to meet its own, ever more insistent needs?

9. Sir Thomas Browne, "Hydriotaphia," in *Religio Medici and Other Works*, ed. L. C. Martin (Oxford: Clarendon Press, 1964), 123.

A TWILIGHT INDUSTRY

1. Vayson de Pradenne bequeathed his entire collection of mallets to the Musée d'Apt, where it can be seen today.

2. Vayson de Pradenne, "L'industrie des ateliers à maillets de Murs," *Journal du Congrès préhistorique de Provence*, 1931: 146–179.

STELAE

1. André d'Anna, *Les statues-menhirs et stèles anthropomorphes du midi méditerranéen* (Paris: Editions du CNRS, 1977), 233.

2. Jacques Cauvin, *Naissance des divinités, naissance de l'agriculture: La ré-*

volution des symboles au Néolithique (Paris: Editions du CNRS, 1994), 100. My translation.

3. Ibid., 100. See page 268 of this marvelous study in which Cauvin speaks of "humanity's transformation of the world at large, carrying within its structure, divided now between the human and the divine, each and every existential malaise along with all that implies of impatience, material progress and future accelerations in a framework, now, of historic time." My translation.

ECHOES IN CLAY

1. Michel Py, *Les Gaulois du Midi: De la fin de l'Age du Bronze à la conquête romaine* (Paris: Hachette, 1993), 78.

2. Ibid., 71.

3. Alain Mendoza, "À propos de quelques décors mailhaciens de Camp Redon I," in *Archéologie en Languedoc: Hommages à Henri Prades* (Lattes: Fédération archéologique de l'Hérault, 1990), 93–95.

BABY BURIALS

1. Bernard Dedet, Henri Duday, and Anne-Marie Tillier, "Inhumations de foetus, nouveau-nés et nourrissons dans les habitats protohistoriques du Languedoc: L'exemple de Gailhan (Gard)," *Gallia* 48 (1991): 96. I have drawn virtually all my field information for the present essay from this meticulous, exhaustive study on the subject. I hereby wish to express my profound gratitude to its authors; also, to Jean Simon, *l'inventeur* of the site of Gailhan, who graciously led me up to the *oppidum* itself, overrun today in boxwood and juniper and visited by little more, each winter, than families of marauding boars.

2. Ibid, 96.

3. Ibid, 102.

4. Py, *Les Gaulois du Midi*, 149.

5. Ibid, 77.

6. Ibid, 144.

TERREMARE

1. Henri Prades, Bernard Dedet, and Michel Py, "*L'occupation des rivages de l'Etang de Mauguio (Hérault) au Bronze Final et au Premier Age du Fer*," 3 vols. (Caveirac: A.R.A.L.O., 1985).

ON THE LONGEVITY OF TOPONYMS

1. V. Bertoldi, "Problèmes de substrat," *Bulletin de la Société de Linguistique* 32 (1931): 93–184.

2. P. Fouché, "Quelques considérations sur la 'base' toponymique: A propos du pré-indo-européen KAL-," *Revue des Langues Romanes* 63 (1939): 295–326.

3. Charles Rostaing's study *Les noms de lieux* (Paris: Presses Universitaires de France, 1972) and his authoritative treatise *Essai sur la toponymie de la Provence (depuis les origines jusqu'aux invasions barbares)* (Paris: Editions D'Artrey, 1950) have both been indispensable sources of information for this essay.

4. Rostaing, *Les noms de lieux*, 13.

5. Auguste Vincent, *Toponymie de la France* (Brussels: Librairie générale, 1937), 496.

6. Both Frédéric Mistral and D. Fletcher Valls are cited in Fernand Benoit, *Recherches sur l'hellénisation du Midi de la Gaule* (Aix-en-Provence: Publications des Annales de la Faculté des Lettres, Editions Ophrys, 1965), 130 n. 58.

7. Even if *Iberi* was the name given by both Greek and Roman authors since the sixth century B.C. to designate a people living alongside the Mediterranean between the Strait of Gibraltar and the mouth of the Rhone, the origin of this nominative is earlier, and—almost certainly—native to that indigenous culture itself.

THE CULT OF SKULLS

1. Strabo, *Geographica*, 4.4.5.

2. Diodorus Siculus, *Biblioteca historica*, 34.23.

3. Nora Chadwick, cited by François Salviat, "La sculpture d'Entremont," in *Archéologie d'Entremont au Musée Granet* (Aix-en-Province: Association des Amis du Musée Granet, 1993), 212.

4. Roland Coignard and Olivier Coignard, "L'ensemble lapidaire de Roque-pertuse: Nouvelle approche," in *Roquepertuse et les Celto-Ligures*, *Documents d'archéologie méridionale* 14 (1991): 39.

5. Fernand Benoit, "L'art primitif mediterranéen de la vallée du Rhone: La sculpture" (Paris: Vanoest, 1945).

6. André Varagnac, cited by Salviat, "La sculpture d'Entremont," 213.

7. Brigitte Lescure, *Voyage en Massalie* (Marseilles: Edisud, 1990), 166.

NEGATIVE ARCHITECTURE

1. Strabo, *Geographica*, 4.1.6

UNDULANT-OBLIQUE

1. Here and throughout, I feel greatly indebted to Benoit's seminal work, *Recherches sur l'hellénisation du Midi de la Gaule.*

2. Heraclitus, fragment 59, cited in *Ancilla to the Pre-Socractic Philosophers: A Complete Translation of the Fragment in Diels, Fragmente der Vorsokratiker*, ed. and trans. Kathleen Freeman (Cambridge, Mass.: Harvard University Press, 1956), 28. Translation by Freeman.

3. Ibid., fragment 41. My translation.

4. Ibid., fragment 51. My translation.

5. Emile Benveniste, *Problèmes de linguistique générale* (Paris: Gallimard, 1966), 1:333. My translation.

6. Charles Olsen, "Projective Verse," in *Selected Writings*, ed. Robert Creeley (New York: New Directions, 1966), 16.

7. Henri Maldiney, "L'esthétique des rythmes," in *Regard, parole, espace* (Lausanne: Editions L'âge d'homme, 1973), 158. My translation.

8. Friedrich Schiller, *Tabulae votivae*, as quoted by G.W.F. Hegel in his introduction to *Einleitung in die Ästhetik*. Cited by Maldiney, "L'esthétique des rythmes," 147. My translation.

TRACKING HANNIBAL

1. Livy, *Ab urbe condita*, 21.22.6.

2. Ibid., 21.35.4.

3. Maurice Herzog, in his preface to Francis de Coninck, *Hannibal à travers les Alpes* (Montélimar: Editions Ediculture, 1992), 3.

4. Polybius, *Historiae*, 3.36.3.

5. Valerius Maximus, *Facta et dicta memorabilia*, 1.7.6.

6. As noted by Dennis Proctor, *Hannibal's March in History* (Oxford: Clarendon Press, 1971), 7.

7. Zonaras, citing a lost work by Dion Cassius in his *Annales* (Basel, 1557), 8.23.

8. According to Paul Marquion, this staging area had to cover an expanse of at least three hundred hectares (three million square meters). See Paul Marquion, "Sur les pas d'Annibal," *Bulletin des amis d'Orange*, no.12 (1963): 9–14.

9. Hannibal's victory against the Gauls, that day, would cost him no less than ten thousand lives.

10. Proctor, *Hannibal's March in History*, 199.

11. Marc Bloch, *Apologie pour l'histoire; ou Métier d'historien* (Paris: Librairie Armand Colin, 1949), 23. Quoted by Paul Jal in his introduction to *Histoire romaine de Tite-Live*, book 21 (Paris: Société d'édition Les Belles Lettres, 1988), lviii. My translation.

12. Ulrich Kahrstedt, *Geschichte der Karthager von 218–146* (Berlin: Weidmann, 1913), 181.

WHAT THE THUNDER SAID

1. Lucan, *Pharsalia*, 1.606–609. Quoted in Marcel Leglay, "Fulgur Conditu: Un lieu consacré par la foudre en Grande-Kabylie," *Libyca* 7 (1959): 101–109.

2. Plutarch, *Quaestiones conviviales*, 4.2-3. Quoted in Leglay, "Fulgur Conditu."

3. Sigmund Freud, "The Antithetical Sense of Primal Words," in *Collected Papers*, trans. Joan Riviere (London: The Hogarth Press,), 4:188, 191.

4. The material within this paragraph has been drawn from Georges Dumézil, *Fêtes romaines d'été et d'automne* (Paris: Gallimard, 1975), most especially from "Le blé et le vin," 83–107.

5. Pliny the Elder, *Naturalis historia*, 2.56: "quinque altius pedibus descendit in terram."

6. Eliade, *Traité d'histoire des religions*, 79–80.

7. See Leglay, "Fulgur Conditu," 101–109.

AERIA THE EVANESCENT

1. Strabo, *Geographica*, 4.1.11. My translation. This is the only antique text that actually describes Aeria. As such, it has been an endless source of both curiosity and confusion for those who have attempted to locate the lost city itself.

2. Alexandre Chevalier, *Le site d'Aeria* (Valence: Imprimeries Réunies, 1968), 43. My translation.

3. Apollodorus, *Chronicles*, 4, fragment 24. My translation.

4. Strabo, *Geographica*, 4.1.11.

5. Pliny the Elder, *Naturalis historia*, 3.4.36.

6. Chevalier, *Le site d'Aeria*, 69. My translation.

7. Ernest Herzog, *Galliae narbonensis; provinciae romanae historia descriptio institutorum expositio* (Leipzig: Tuebner, 1864), 28. Quoted by Guy Barruol in his excellent study, "A la recherche d'Aeria, ville celtique," *Latomus* 31 (1972): 971.

VOTIVE MIRRORS

1. From a *parthenion* or choral lyric written by Pindar and cited in the *scholium* or commentary on Theocritus, 2.10.

2. Guy Barruol, "Miroirs votifs découverts en Provence et dédiés à Sélènè et à Aphroditè," *Revue archéologique de Narbonnaise* 18 (1985): 372. My translation. Barruol's excellent study has been the source for nearly all the archeological data cited in the present essay. I hereby wish to express my profound gratitude to Monsieur Barruol for this study in particular and his immense contribution to Provençal archeology in general.

DREAM INCUBATION

1. Claude Bourgeois, *Divona* (Paris: Editions DeBoccard, 1991), 1:242. My translation.

2. Henri Lechat, "Incubatio," in Charles Daremberg and Edmond Saglio, *Dictionnaire des antiquités, grecques et romaines* (Paris: Hachette, 1877–1919), vol. 3:1, pp. 458–460. My translation.

LE PONT FLAVIEN

1. It is in the outskirts of present-day Saint-Chamas (Bouches-du-Rhône).

2. Anne Roth-Congès, "Le Pont Flavien de Saint-Chamas: Architecture Augustéenne en Provence" (Ph.D. diss., Université de Provence, Aix-en-Provence, 1981), 232–233.

3. Ibid., 253.

4. Martin Heidegger, "Bauen Wohnen Denken," in *Vorträge und Aufsätze* (Pfullingen: G. Neske, 1954). My translation.

5. Ibid. My translation.

1. Jean-Luc Fiches and Jean-Louis Paillet, "Prospections et fouilles: Archéologie d'un aqueduc," in *L'aqueduc de Nîmes et le Pont Du Gard* (Nimes: Conseil Général du Gard/CNRS, 1991), 252.

2. Vitruvius, *De architectura*, 8.4.1. My translation.

3. Alain Malissard, *Les Romains et l'eau* (Paris: Realia/Les Belles Lettres, 1994), 18. My translation.

4. Cicero, *Ad Atticum*, 2.1.8.

5. Vitruvius, *De architectura*, 8.6.1. My translation.

6. Philippe Leveau, "L'aqueduc de Nîmes et les aqueducs antiques," in *L'aqueduc de Nîmes et le Pont Du Gard*, 245. The phrase in its entirety reads: "*Monument typiquement urbain par sa finalité, rural par son tracé, l'aqueduc apparaît comme un excellent symbole de la romanité.*"

7. Pliny the Elder, *Naturalis historia*, 36.58.

8. Malissard, *Les Romains*, 177. My translation.

9. Jean-Jacques Rousseau, *Les confessions*, book 6. Quoted in Malissard, *Les Romains*, 178. My translation.

10. Albert Grenier, *Manuel d'archéologie gallo-romaine* (Paris: Editions Picard, 1960), 226. My translation.

11. Malissard, *Les Romains*, 268. My translation.

Index

Page numbers in italics refer to illustrations.

Casaubon, Isaac, 155

Cassis, 113

Cauvin, Jacques, 77, 226n.3

Cavares, 168

cave paintings, 19–20

celestial father / terrestrial mother, 163, 164

Celto-Iberian civilization, 108

Celto-Ligurians, 114–15, 121–27

Celts, 98; cities of, 170; incineration of dead by, 107–8; language of, 113, 114, 171; mythology of, 124, 164, *165;* social structure/skills of, 121; southeastern France infiltrated by, 114, 121

ceramics: Corinthian pottery, 109; Corsican, 31; impressed ware, 31; Ionico-Massalian pottery, 137–39, *140,* 141–44; Ligurian, 31; Mailhacien pottery, 84, *85,* 87–91, *88;* motifs in, 84, *85,* 138, *140,* 141–44; and number/measurement, 36; Rhodian, 108; and settling of populations, 30; Spanish, 31; terremare, 104, *105,* 106, 111

Cézanne, Paul, 141–42

Chastelard-Lardiers, 187–90, *191,* 192–93

Chateaubriand, 203

Chellean people, 14

Chelles, 15

Chevalier, Alexandre, 172

chieftains, 49, 98

Childe, V. Gorden, 34–35

chorobate (surveyor's table), 207–8

Christendom / Christianity, 115, 126

Cicero, 207

circitores (maintenance workers), 217

cities, ancient, and farmland, 170

civilization and image, 127

clandestins (treasure seekers), 49, 190, 192

Claudius, 215, 222

cobbles, paleogeologic study of, 15

Coelius Antipater, 149, 150

coffers, terra-cotta (Trets, Var), 71

Col de Larche (Alps), 156

Colonia Julia Augusta Apolloinaris Reiorm, 183

concept, as an order of thought, 143

Corinthian pottery, 108

Corsica, 31

Courtin, Jean, 56

Crach tomb pictograph (Morbihan), 48

cremation (incineration), 99, 100

Cro-Magnon, 18–19

culture, as material, 51

cuttlefish frescoes (Knossos palace, Crete), 48

Cuttlefish of Lufang pictograph (Crach tomb, Morbihan), 48

Cypriots, 160

Helios, 177

Heraclitus, 43, 138, 139

Hermes-Mercury, 182

Herodotus, 137–38

Herzog, Ernest, 172

Historiae (Polybius), 147–48, 149, 150, 151, 152–53

history: gaps in, 145–46, 156–57; as survival of artifacts, 49–50

Homo faber, 11, 13

Homo habilis, 13

Homo neanderthalensis, 16–17, 122–23

Homo sapiens sapiens (Cro-Magnon), 18–19

human advancement, 91

human evolution, 16, 18

human face, representation of, 70

human figuration, birth of, 70–71, 73, 76, 77

humanism, 142

human migrations, 19, 33–34, 60

human progress, 225n.5

hunters, 19, 26–28

hunting/gathering to farming/ stockbreeding, 75

Hypnos, 184

hypogea. *See* burial sites

ibère, 119

Iberi, 227n.7

Iberia, 119

Iberian alphabet, 89

Ile de la Barthelasse, 154

Ile de la Piboulette, 154

Ile du Malatras, 154

incineration, 99, 100

incubatio (dream incubation), 180–86

infant burials (Languedoc), 93–97, 99–100, 226n.1

infanticide, 95

inhumation. *See* burial sites; skeletons

intelligence, auroral, 138

interval, humans as creatures of, 20

Ionian pottery, 109

Ionians, 137–39

Ionico-Massalian pottery, 137–39, *140,* 141–44

Iovo Frugifero (Jupiter), 162. *See also* Jupiter

iridescent chaos, 141–42

iron, use of, 48–49, 90

Iron Age: class structure during, 98; infant burials in, 93–97, 99–100, 226n.1; infant mortality in, 95; market economy of, 97–98, 110; technological development during, 91, 97; transition from Bronze Age, 90–91, 99; warrior cultures of, 98, 99, 124. *See also* terremare (Languedoc)

Iupiter Fulgerator (Jupiter), 161, 162. *See also* Jupiter

Iupiter Tonans (Jupiter), 161. *See also* Jupiter

Jacob, 181

Jardin des Vestiges (Marseilles), 136

javelin points, 21, 23

Jupiter, 158, 161–63

Jupiter Optimus Maximus, 161

Jupiter sculpture (Zaghouan, Tunisia), 163

Kahrstedt, Ulrich, 157

kal, 114

kar-, 113

Klee, Paul, 141

Knossos cuttlefish frescoes (Crete), 48

L'Abri de la Font-des-Pigeons (Châteauneuf-les-Martigues), 30, 223n.1

La Chapelle-aux-Saints burial site, 18

La Cloche skulls/sculptures, 122, 126

La Escudilla (Valencia), 96

Lagozzians, 73

La Madeleine, 15

land surveyors, 205, 207–8, 210

languages, 113; and birth of alphabets, 49, 84, 89; Celtic, 113, 114, 171;

French, 113; Greek, 89, 114–15, 171, 178; Latin, 113; Provençal, 113

Languedoc: infant burial site at, 93–97, 99–100, 226n.1; marshlands of, 101–2, 111; moors of, 208; tombs at, 61. *See also* terremare (Languedoc)

La Pointe de l'Arquet quarries (La Couronne), 131–36, *132*

Latin language, 113

Lauris-Puyvert stele, *72*

Lauzet-Ubaye tomb, *59*

Le Cayla-de-Mailhac (Aude), 86, 90

Leglay, Marcel, 164

Le Mas-D'Azil skull, 123

Le Moustier, 15

Leroi-Gourhan, André, 47

Les Collines de Cordes, 45–48, *46, 49*–50

Lescure, Brigitte, 124

Lez, 169

libratores (land surveyors), 205, 207–8, 210

libri fulgurales (Etruscan oracular books), 160–61, 163

Licinios Touteinos, Q., 177

life and death, 56–57

lightning, as awe-inspiring, 166

lightning worship, Gallo-Roman, 158–61; and conceptions of Jupiter, 163; *Fulgur Conditum* inscriptions,

moiety societies, 87

Mommsen, Theodor, 155

Monts de Vaucluse, 64–65, 66

monument and metaphor, 215, 218, 222

moon imagery, Neolithic, 48, 49, 50, 225n.8

Mousterian, 18

Mousterian skull (Grotto of Guattari, Mount Circe, Italy), 122–23

Mureybet skulls, 123

Musée Granet (Aix-en-Provence), 126

Napoleon, 155

Naturalis historia (Pliny the Elder), 163, 171–72, 213

nature: vs. abstraction, 49; control of, 75, 77–78, 225n.8; elusiveness of, 43–44; humankind's contract with, 28–29; rupture with, 75–76

naves lapidariae, 133–34

Neanderthal. See *Homo neander-thalensis*

negative architecture, 131–36

Neolithic people: afterlife for, 56–57, 62; as agrarian, 25, 30, 34, 57, 60–61; decline of, 66–67; dwellings of, 58; fetal-position burial by, 57; fishing by, 32; flint extraction by, 64–69; and food-production in-crease, 35; as harnassing nature, 225n.8; hierarchies among, 60; in-fant burial among, 97; migration of, 33–34, 60; moon imagery of, 48, 49, 50, 225n.8; and number/measurement, 36; population in-crease among, 35; Pradenne on, 67; in Provence, as water oriented, 31–32; rebirth/regeneration symbols of, 47, 48, 61–62; as sedentary, 60; skulls used for ancestor worship by, 123; sun imagery of, 48–49, 61–62, 225n.8; tombs of, 58, *59,* 60–62, 225n.5; warfare among, 35. *See also* stelae, Neolithic

Neolithic period vs. postindustrial age, material culture of, 67–68

Neolithic Revolution, 34–35, 60, 75

Nice, 10, 11

Nicolas, Hector, 40, 44

Nietzsche, Friedrich Wilhelm, 141

Nîmes, 146, 205, 218, 222

Nîmes altar, 164–66, *165*

Nîmes aqueduct. *See* aqueduct (Nîmes)

number/measurement, 36, 142

oil refineries, 116, 117, 119–20

Oldowan people, 14

Olson, Charles, 141

oneiromancers (dream priests), 180,
181, 184

oppidum (Barri), 169–70

opus signinum (mortar), 213

Orange, 113, 168, 170

orthostats, 58

ossuaries, 99

pagus, 170

Palasgi, 160

paleobotanists, 16

paleogeologists, 15

Paleolithic period, 11, 18, 123;
fecundity / regeneration symbols
of, 47–48; human migrations
during, 19

Papago Indians (Arizona), 87

passage, 197–99

patriarchies, 49

pax romana, 171

petrol refineries, 116, 117, 119–20

Pheonicians, 137, 160

philosophy, evolution of, 142

pictographs: vs. alphabets, 49; Cuttlefish of Lufang, 48; on Mailhacien
pottery, 84, *85,* 87–91, *88; U-*
shaped, 45–48, *46,* 49–50

pilgrimages, 188–89

Pindar, 177

place, value of, 198

place names. *See* toponyms

Plato, 142

Pleiades, 147, 155

Pliny the Elder, *Naturalis historia,*
163, 171–72, 213

Plutarch, 160

poem, as high-energy construct, 141

pollen, fossilized, 16

pollution, 117–18

Polybius, 146; *Historiae,* 147–48, 149,
150, 151, 152–53

Pont Flavien, 194–99, *195–96,* 231n.1

portraiture, 78

Pradenne, Vayson de, 65–68

prayer, 192–93

predation to production, 75

Proctor, Dennis, 155

Prometheus, 76

Provençal language, 113

Provence: deposit layers in, 3; game
in, 27–28; historians in, 4; icy
ground in, 61; poignancy of, 5;
tombs in, 61 (*see also* tombs); wind
in, 5, 11

Provincia Romana, 115

Ptolemy, 171

Py, Michel, 86, 89, 97–98, 99

Quaternary period, 14, 15

questions, 54–55

Schiller, Friedrich von, 143

Scipio, Publius Cornelius, 151

scows, for transporting stone, 133–34

seashell ear (Roque d'Aille, Var),
52–55, *53*

Second Punic War, 145, 147–48

Selene, 174, 176–77

self-duplication, 88

self-recognition / self-realization,
19–20, 75–78

Seneca, 203

Shell Petroleum, 119–20

silence, degrees of, 149

Silenus, 148–49

skeletons: at Avignon, 32, *33;* in fetal
position, 57, 94–95; first, 18; at La
Chapelle-aux-Saints, 18; Neolithic
vs. Medieval, 225n.5; and ritual
burial, 18–19; at Uzbekistan, 18–19.
See also burial sites; skulls

skulls: in ancestor worship, 123–24;
Celto-Ligurian cult of, 121–27;
at Entremont, 122, 126; at Grotto
of Guattari, 122–23; and headhunting, 123–24; at La Cloche, 122;
at Le Mas-D'Azil, 123; magico-
religious treatment of, 123–24; at
Mureybet, 123; at Roque d'Aille,
52–55, *53;* at Roquepertuse, 122.
See also skeletons

solar-funereal mythologies, 61–62

Somnus, 183–84, *185*

soul and beauty, 179

Spanish ceramics, 31

speculation, 179

speculum, 179

spring, curative (Riez, Alpes-de-
Haute-Provence), 182–83

stelae, Neolithic, 70–71, *72,* 73–78;
genitalia represented in, 73–74;
geometric-patterned hair of, 71, 73;
the mouth's absence from, 74; and
religiosity, 74–75; and self-recognition, 77, 78

Stone Age, 65

Strabo, 121, 133, 134; *Geographica,*
167, 168–69, 170, 230n.1

sun imagery, Neolithic, 48–49, 61–62,
225n.8

Taffanel, Jean, 89

Taffanel, Odile, 89

Tain, 124

tar, 113

Taranis, 164, *165*

Tarascon, 113

Tarquinius, Priscus, 161

Tarquinius, Superbus, 161

technological development vs. human
advancement, 91

temples: at Epidaurus, 182; offerings at, 189 (*see also* Chastelard-Lardiers; votive mirrors); at Riez, 182–84, 186

temporal vs. spatial, 35–36

Terra Amata windbreak (Nice), 9–12, *10*

terra-cotta votive lamps, 188–89, 192

terremare (Languedoc), 102–11; abandonment of, 109–10; altitude of, 103–4; ceramic ware / pottery of, 104, *105*, 106, 111; cinerary urns of, 108; continual, seasonal occupation of, 104–6, 109; cultural influx at, 108–9; daubed wall of, 106; displacement of artifacts of, 104; dwellings of, 106–7; irrigation ditches of, 111; marginalization of, 109–10; and marshland reclamation, 107; as situated along watercourses, 103, 108; strata of, 104–5

thermoluminescent analysis, 51

Thomsen, Christian, 91

Three Age System, 91

tin, 117

tombs: Neolithic, 58, *59*, 60–62, 225n.5; orientation of corridors to, 61–62

toponyms, 112–16, 119–20, 148, 171

topos, 171

Touloubre, 197

trading posts, 137

transcendence, 199

translation, 62–63

travertine concretions, 217, 219–20

treasure hunters, 49, 190, 192

Trets terra-cotta coffers (Var), 71

Tricastini, 170

tufa, 217

Tunisian Jupiter sculpture, 163

typometric diagrams, 42–43

undulant pattern, in pottery, 138–39, *140*, 142–44

Urnfield, 107–8

Uzbekistan burial site, 18–19

Uzès, 205

Valerius Maximus, 149

Vallon des Vergiers (Murs), 64, 68

Valls, D. Fletcher, 119

Van Gogh, Vincent, 5

Venetian Lagoon, 103

Via Iberia (later Via Domitia), 146

Vinalia priora, 162

Vincent, Auguste, 119

Visigoths, 117, 218

Vitruvius, 205, 212

Volcae, 146, 150

votive contract, 176

votive lamps, terra-cotta, 188, 192

votive mirrors, 174–79, *175*

vulvaforms (*U*-shaped pictographs), 45–48, *46*, 49–50

warfare, Neolithic, 35

water: quality of, 204–5, 212; as sacred/magical, 206, 207

watercress, 119

waters, curative (Riez, Alpes-de-Haute-Provence), 182–83

water-tapping, 215–16

wave motif, in pottery, 138–39, *140*, 141–44

wildlife, as bountiful, 28

wind, 5, 11

windbreak (Terra Amata, Nice), 9–12, *10*

wine, 108, 137, 162

women in love, votive offerings of, 177

words, 68, 162

writing, birth of, 84, 89

Würm phase (Quarternary epoch), 15

Xenophon, 151

Zeus, 182

Zeus Keraunos, 160

Zonaras, 152

zoomorphic motifs, *85*

Text: 10.75/16 Fournier
Display: Fournier and Gill Sans Bold
Design: Nicole Hayward
Composition: Integrated Composition Systems
Printing and binding: Rose Printing Company, Inc.